ELITE UNITS

OF THE THIRD REICH

German Special Forces in World War II

ELITE UNITS
OF THE THIRD REICH
German Special Forces in World War II

TIM RIPLEY

LEWIS

INTERNATIONAL, INC.

First published in the United States in 2002 by
Lewis International, Inc.
Copyright © 2002 The Brown Reference Group plc

Lewis International, Inc.
2201 N.W. 102 Place, #1
Miami, F1 33172 USA

Tel: 305-436-7984 / 800-259-5962
Fax: 305-436-7985 / 800-664-5095

ISBN 1-930983-16-6

Editorial and Design:
The Brown Reference Group plc
8 Chapel Place
Rivington Street
London
EC2A 3DQ
UK
www.brownreference.com

Printed in Hong Kong

Editors: Peter Darman, Tony Hall
Picture Research: Andrew Webb
Design: Wilson Design Associates
Production: Matt Weyland

CONTENTS

Introduction

Adolf Hitler's soldiers proved to be some of the most fearsome fighting men of the twentieth century. In the first three years of World War II (1939–42) they surged forward from one victory to another and then, as the tide turned against the Third Reich, they fought doggedly in an effort to delay inevitable defeat. The Führer's best technicians, generals, soldiers, sailors and airmen were often syphoned off into the Third Reich's elite units – expert fighters equipped with technologically advanced hardware.

By 1942, Adolf Hitler had carved out a European empire from the Atlantic coast to the Russian steppes. However, he knew he was surrounded by undefeated enemies and feared disloyalty. For these reasons he put his faith increasingly in ideological and technical elites.

At the height of the Third Reich in the autumn of 1942, Adolf Hitler's armies had advanced to the banks of the River Volga, were pushing towards Cairo, dominated the Balkans and occupied western Europe from the Pyrenees to the Arctic, while German submarines were sinking ships off America's Atlantic Coast. Within three years the Führer's "Thousand Year Reich" was in ruins: Soviet troops were raising the Red Flag above the rubble of Berlin before linking up with Allied troops advancing from the Rhine.

Hitler's first reaction to the string of defeats after the failure of the German Army to take Moscow in the winter of 1941 was to begin to form special, ultra-loyal elite units to reinvigorate his flagging armies. The Führer was convinced his generals lacked the necessary will to fight the total war, so he turned to the Waffen-SS and a small number of hand-picked army units to fight to the death. They lived up to their Führer's faith and fought with fanaticism, in the face of massive odds.

At the same time, Hitler was convinced that Germany's scientists and engineers could provide him with the answer to his problems and win the war. Special units were formed to take these weapons into battle, with the best pilots, missile experts, tank crews and submariners grouped together in elite units. They were the Third Reich's technical elite, and were some of the first warriors in military history to rely on science rather than simply martial prowess to defeat their enemies.

Whenever Allied or Soviet soldiers met their German opponents in battle, they found them determined, skillful and deadly opponents. In the deserts of North Africa, the skies of Europe, on the Russian steppe, out in the stormy Atlantic, Italy's mountains or the hedgerows of Normandy, Germany's warriors always put up a "hell of a fight".

Many of Nazi Germany's elite units earned themselves legendary status for their martial prowess. Units like the Waffen-SS *Leibstandarte Adolf Hitler* Panzer Division, Waffen-SS foreign legions or Admiral Karl Dönitz's U-boat fleet showed amazing battlefield bravery in the face of

overwhelming odds. Their losses were staggering, yet time after time they returned to the fight, even when they knew the war was lost.

Some of Hitler's top units, such as the *Grossdeutschland* Division, were successful in battle due to the sheer professionalism of their soldiers and the efficient organization and effective leadership of their officers. These were men who took soldiering very seriously. Kurt Student's paratroopers and Erwin Rommel's 7th Panzer Division were not only professional outfits, but pioneered new forms of warfare – airborne and armoured. They revolutionized war with their trailblazing Blitzkrieg tactics that conquered Europe for Hitler.

Other Nazi units took on elite status because they were equipped with the best and most advanced hardware available. Units with Tiger tanks or 88mm flak guns were considered battle-winning weapons and always led the attack or formed the bulwark of a defensive position. They had to used in battle by the best men available. Hitler believed passionately that so-called "wonder weapons" could win

Opposite top: General Erwin
Rommel, victor in France in 1940 and
a genius in the art of armoured
warfare. His rise to prominence was
due to his ability to give Adolf Hitler
what he desired most: action, results
and victories.

Opposite bottom: General Kurt
Student. The innovator behind
Germany's airborne arm, he was one
of its greatest commanders.

Right: An armoured column of
panzergrenadiers advances into
Russia during Operation Barbarossa,
1941. Hitler envisaged the best of his
army to be steadfast, ideologically
driven soldiers fighting with the very
best equipment military technology
could devise.

Germany the war. He took this to the extreme when he pumped men
and materiel into the "Vengeance Weapon" programme. In doing so he
created a new elite of techno-warriors.

As Hitler's Third Reich fell apart under the relentless pressure of
Allied attacks, a new breed of elite unit came to the fore – those formed
around charismatic, dashing and ruthless leaders. Men like Otto
Skorzeny, Hans-Ulrich Rudel and Adolf Galland led units that will be
forever identified with their names. These men were all personal
favourites of Hitler. As the Führer became ever more disillusioned with
the army's generals who brought him nothing but defeat after defeat,
these men only provided him with good news. He showered them
with medals, publicity and let them indulge their every whim. On the
battlefield they were fearless, determined and skillful leaders.

The prowess of the German armed forces was not due to one single factor but a number of them. Hitler enjoyed the benefit of inheriting the highly professional German officer corps when he seized power in 1933. Germany's General Staff Corps was at the heart of the country's rearmament programme during the 1930s, and it moulded the expanded Wehrmacht into a highly professional organization. Officers, noncommissioned officers (NCOs) and soldiers were all trained to a very high standard, which meant German units went into battle prepared for every eventuality. This became increasing important as the war turned against Hitler and outnumbered German units had to stage determined rearguard actions against overwhelming odds.

For its time, Hitler's Wehrmacht was very advanced. It was keen to adopt the latest technology and management procedures, giving it a vital edge over its more pedestrian opponents. The Germans, for example, were quick to field Blitzkrieg tactics based on the aggressive use of tanks, paratroopers, close air support and huge fleets of motor vehicles. At the same time the Germans took quickly to using radios to command and control all their operations, which meant they could be conducted at a pace and tempo previously unknown in military history.

QUALITY VERSUS NUMBERS

Germany's advanced industrial base meant that the Führer was able to provide his fighting men with weapons that were generally far superior to those available to their opponents. Weapon for weapon, the products of the Messerschmitt, Henschel, Krupp and Heinkel companies were more than a match for the anything the British, French, Russians or Americans could produce. The Tiger tank, 88mm flak gun and Me 262 jet fighter have all entered military history as "classic" weapons. The high quality of these weapons, however, turned into the Third Reich's Achilles' heel because the quest to produce superior weapons meant they were far more expensive and difficult to produce than those of the Soviets or Allies. In the end, Germany's enemies proved able to out-produce her and massed overwhelming force on the battlefields of Europe.

Hitler was fortunate to rule one of the best educated countries in Europe. The manpower the Führer's generals had to work with was far superior to that available to their opponents. While every German soldier was literate and most officers were university graduates, the Soviet Red Army had little more than illiterate peasants to draw on. As a result, German soldiers were not dependent on their senior officers and could keep fighting if they found themselves leaderless. The Germans taught their officers and soldiers to fight according to the principles of mission command, so if a commander was killed his second-in-command could take over and still complete the mission. Commanders were given objectives to be achieved and

left to complete their task, rather than being given specific instructions on how to do the job.

Outnumbered and sometimes surrounded, it was often only down to the fighting spirit of beleaguered German soldiers and the leadership provided by a few determined officers that kept the Führer's armies fighting. There was no magic ingredient to the motivation of Germany's soldiers.

Underlying every action of Hitler's armies was the indoctrination of the German nation from 1933 to believe that Germans were racially superior to all other peoples, particularly Slavs and Jews. Hitler convinced his people that they were the "herrenvolk", or master race, who were destined to rule over inferior "untermenschen" or sub-humans. Relentless propaganda was pumped out by Propaganda Minister Josef Goebbels that the German people were embarked upon a total war to ensure the survival of their race. As the war intensified and German cities were reduced to ruins by Allied bombing, the sense of total war became real. On the Eastern Front, the German policy of exterminating Jews, random killing of civilians and systematic starvation of prisoners of war turned the war into a ruthless struggle. German soldiers rapidly became aware that no quarter would be given to them

The Ju 87 Stuka was a prime example of a weapon which was given years of extra operational life by continual technological development. The Stuka first flew in 1935: it was still fighting 10 years later.

The ability of Hitler's regime to mobilize and train huge numbers of men capable of fighting with technologically advanced weapons of war – such as these U-boats – stunned the world in the 1940s.

if they fell into Soviet hands, so surrender was not an option. For German soldiers facing enemies at the front and bombing at home, it was apparent that victory was the only way for them and their country to survive.

For a hard core of Nazis in the Waffen-SS and other services, there were other motivations for winning the war. Many owed their positions and wealth to the Führer and his regime. They had grown rich and powerful during the Nazis' rise to power. As the German Blitzkrieg surged through Europe, there were rich pickings for senior Nazis and army officers. Castles, art treasures and all the other trappings of imperial glory were on offer from a grateful Führer to his loyal subordinates.

The German Army had more than 200 years of tradition to fall back on in moments of adversity. Although the Imperial German Army had been disbanded at the end of the World War I, the leadership traditions of the German officer corps lived on in the Reichswehr in the 1920s, and then the Wehrmacht. Aristocratic officers may have been in the minority in the Führer's army, but the ones that remained continued to adhere to an age-old military ethos. They put the welfare of their men before themselves and led from the front. In return, the rank and file loyally stuck by their officers in times of crisis.

Experience taught the Wehrmacht to keep their men together in the same unit as long as possible to ensure they bonded as a team. Units would be raised in a specific town or region, trained together, then sent into battle together. As a result, they fought to protect their comrades, just as much they fought for their country.

In the shadows of the collapsing Reich, many German soldiers became aware that their country was a repressive police state. Rumours of the concentration camps were widespread, but after the July 1944 bomb plot against Hitler, the Führer unleashed his terror on the Wehrmacht itself. Thousands of suspects were arrested and hundreds executed as the hunt for traitors in its ranks ran out of control. Nazi Party officials and SS officers took over key command posts, and the remaining officers were acutely aware that the slightest deviance from the Führer's orders would result in severe repercussions. For the rank and file, there were field court martials that sent thousands of men to firing squads or the hangman's noose if they showed insufficient fighting spirit.

This book tells the story of Nazi Germany's elite units. It profiles the German Army, Air Force, Navy and Waffen-SS units that were in the vanguard of Hitler's murderous war of conquest, and looks closely at the men, their weapons, equipment, leaders, tactics, victories and defeats.

There was a tendency for German military scientists to concentrate on creating ever larger and more powerful machines. German panzers increased in size from the 9-tonne (8-ton) Panzer II in 1939 to the 58-tonne (57-ton) Tiger I (below) three years later.

7th Panzer Division – Ghost Division

The 7th Panzer Division fought throughout World War II, taking part in the Blitzkriegs in Poland and the West in 1939–40 and then on the Eastern Front. Led by such charismatic leaders as Rommel, its soldiers became some of the finest panzer troops the Third Reich possessed. Nicknamed the "Ghost Division" for its rapid advance through France in 1940, it ended the war as a mere shadow of its former self. As it died its exploits passed into military legend.

A group of dispirited French generals were being paraded in front of Erwin Rommel during the German Blitzkrieg across France in the summer of 1940. They complained to the 7th Panzer Division's commander, who was later to achieve fame as the "Desert Fox", that his tanks would appear from nowhere and then disappear like ghosts. The name stuck and Rommel's elite unit would be known forever as the "Ghost Division" because of its daring and aggressive tactics. It enhanced its reputation as the Wehrmacht's top panzer unit during the campaign in Russia, spearheading Operation Barbarossa in 1941, then fiercely resisting the Soviet drive westwards after mid-1943.

When Hitler set German rearmament in motion during the 1930s, he instinctively backed the production of weapons that were new or appeared to be revolutionary. Tanks, aircraft and paratroopers all caught his attention as innovative ways to avoid repeating the deadlock of World War I. Like a child in a toy shop he famous exclaimed "that's what I want", after seeing tanks for the first time.

Panzer II tanks of the 7th Panzer Division during the Blitzkrieg in France. The Panzer II had come into service in 1936, but by 1939 was found to be under-gunned and was reduced to a reconnaissance role in the 1940 campaign in the West.

A motorcycle reconnaissance unit of the 7th Panzer Division prepares to cross a hastily constructed pontoon bridge over the Moselle River into France, May 1940. The division's commander, General Rommel, is in the peaked cap to the left.

With the Führer's enthusiastic backing, the Wehrmacht began to organize its tanks into panzer divisions and then corps, which would spearhead Germany's wars of aggression. By September 1939 the panzer force boasted some 2000 tanks, assigned to 4 panzer divisions and 4 light divisions. The former boasted a full panzer brigade and a brigade of motorized infantrymen, while the latter had only a regiment of tanks at the most. Flush with victory over Poland in September 1939, Hitler ordered the expansion of light divisions into full panzer divisions in time for the coming attack on the West in the spring of 1940.

Amid frantic efforts in February 1940, Hitler appointed one of his most loyal officers to command the newly formed 7th Panzer Division, which was earmarked to spearhead the invasion of France. Erwin Rommel was a dynamic and impetuous infantry officer, who had won the *Pour le Merite*, Imperial Germany's highest decoration, in Italy during World War I while leading a unit of Stormtroopers. Though he had never served in a tank unit before, Rommel was a tactical genius who had written the definitive book – *Infantry Attacks* –on the infiltration tactics used by the Stormtroopers. Rommel intended to use these tactics during the coming campaign. Central to Rommel's ideas was the need for tanks to be used aggressively to push deep behind enemy lines and totally unbalance his defences. Speed and confusion would

keep the enemy guessing and allow Rommel's panzers to ignore threats to their flank. They could be tied up later after the enemy's resistance was broken, thought Rommel.

To prepare his men for their coming battle, he relentlessly drilled them on how to move quickly across country and maintain the momentum of the advance. Battle plans and drills were rehearsed, weak officers were sacked. He also ensured that the men were indoctrinated with the latest Nazi ideology. An indication of this was given when he first arrived at his new division and greeted his officers with the Nazi, fascist salute, rather than the conventional army version. The 7th Panzer was being honed into a taut, fighting machine. While the human resources of the division were up to scratch, Rommel was worried about the quality of his tanks. He only had one regiment, some 200 tanks, as opposed to the official strength of more than 320, and over half of his tanks were captured Czech 38Ts. They had far lighter armour than the Daimler Benz Panzer IIIs and Krupp Panzer IVs that made up the rest of his tank strength. The 38Ts, however, would prove faster and more reliable that Rommel's German tanks during the hell-for-leather advance across France.

The prearranged battle plan for the invasion of France, Operation Yellow, was activated on 9 May, and within a matter of hours the 7th

A German transport column motors into the French interior, overflown by a Fieseler Fi 156 Storch reconnaissance aircraft. Command of the roads and air superiority were both essential to the success of the Blitzkrieg in the West in 1940.

General Rommel in a command conference with divisional staff, France May/June 1940. The general pushed the 7th Panzer Division across France from the Moselle to Cherbourg and the Channel Coast in a little over six weeks.

Panzer was moving towards its jump-off position on the Belgian border. Heavy air strikes silenced the Belgian Army frontline positions, opening the way for Rommel's panzers to storm forward. At the River Meuse, Rommel pushed his riflemen to cross in rubber boats, but they soon ran into heavy resistance. As they faltered, the general crossed over to their bridgehead and steadied the troops until a pontoon bridge was built to allow the first panzers to cross.

When the tanks reached the French border, they ran into the field fortifications of the Maginot Line. Rather than become bogged down in battle, Rommel ordered his tank crews to start waving white flags from their turrets. Confused, the French defenders let the Germans drive through their lines. Once safely past the hapless Frenchmen, Rommel just ordered them to keep going, leaving the engineers and infantry following on behind to mop up the bunkers.

The 7th Division now began a helter-skelter dash across France. Columns of panzers raced from village to village. As they lazed in their camps, French troops were machine-gunned by passing panzers. One French division drove down a road and passed Rommel's tanks travelling the other way. The panzers swung their turrets and raked the French trucks with deadly fire. Hundreds died and thousands surrendered. Rather than stop to finish off their victims, the panzers were ordered to keep going by Rommel. His tanks were now clocking 56km (35 miles) a day and pushing deep behind enemy lines. If they ran low on petrol, they simply pulled into French petrol stations and filled up.

Not far behind the lead tanks was Rommel in his armoured command halftrack, constantly urging his troops on or radioing for supplies to be brought forward. He was in his element and told one of his officers: "In this war the commander's place is here, right out in front! I don't believe in armchair strategy. Let's leave that to the gentlemen of the General Staff."

The top brass at Wehrmacht headquarters were far from impressed by what they saw as Rommel's recklessness. But the 7th Panzer's commander was not concerned. On 18 May, he issued orders for his division to advance to the Channel at Le Havre. Two days later, 7th Panzer's advance guard clashed for the first time with British troops south of the town of Arras. Rommel was still confident that little could stop his rampage and geared up his panzers to attack again on 21 May. Little did he know that the British were massing tanks and troops to counterattack his dispersed troops. Two British columns pushed south into the 7th Panzer's exposed flank. Outposts of riflemen were quickly scattered and Rommel rushed forward to steady his troops. The division's artillery regiment was being threatened. Heavily armoured Matilda tanks were moving to overrun the guns when Rommel arrived. He formed his batteries into a gun line and concentrated their fire on the British assault troops. Rommel ran from gun to gun, personally directing the fire. He dodged heavy British fire but emerged without a

Panzer IIs race across the open fields of France heading for the Channel coast, May/June 1940. A knocked-out French Renault light tank is in the foreground.

scratch. The general's aide was less fortunate, and was killed as he tried to keep up with his commander. Under a relentless barrage, 28 tanks were knocked out and the British column faltered. Farther east, a second British column was closing on the 7th Panzer's anti-aircraft regiment. A line of German 37mm anti-tank guns was scattered when their shells bounced off the armour of the Matildas. Fortunately for Rommel, a battery of 88mm flak guns were now in the path of the British tanks. These high-velocity weapons were soon wreaking havoc among the Matildas, knocking out eight. With the British columns halted, Rommel now reorganized his 25th Panzer Regiment and sent it forward to counterattack. It sent the British reeling back to their start line and saved the day for the 7th Panzer Division.

The British were in headlong retreat northwards to Dunkirk, where an armada of ships was gathering to evacuate them across the Channel. Rommel's panzers were hard on their heels. His division's first objective was the city of Lille, which was held by a large French garrison. Rather than wait for daylight, Rommel ordered a night attack into the heart of the city, stirring up a hornet's nest. Snipers picked off panzer commanders in their turrets, and Rommel himself was at one point surrounded by French troops. Some quick reversing saved the day and the general's driver got him out of trouble. The German strike totally unhinged the Allied defences, and soon the French First Army was retreating in chaos. Other panzer units were given the job of defeating the British at Dunkirk, while the 7th Panzer was rested in preparation for the push southwards to finish off the French. So far in the campaign the division had captured almost 7000 prisoners and 48 tanks, as well as destroying more than 300 French and British tanks. A grateful Führer

Above: Panzer 38T light tanks in northern France, summer 1940. The Panzer 38T was a Czech tank taken for German Army service after the annexation of Czechoslovakia in March 1939.

Left: Men of the British Expeditionary Force await evacuation from the Dunkirk beaches, 27 May 1940. Outmanoeuvred and outfought by the German Blitzkrieg, the British Army was forced out of Continental Europe in under three weeks.

rewarded Rommel with the Knight's Cross – the first divisional commander to receive the award during the French campaign.

Rommel now drove his division southwards with a vengeance, smashing open the French defences: 7th Panzer was the first German unit to reach the River Seine. The British and French were in headlong retreat. A huge haul of booty fell into the hands of Rommel's troops as his panzers raced towards the sea. French villagers rushed out to feed 7th Panzer's columns, thinking they were British, only to recoil in horror when they found them to be German. Chateaux filled with fine wine and food were captured and abandoned, as Rommel's men never had time to stay in one place for more than a few hours. On 10 June they reached the Channel at Dieppe. When a large British and French force was found embarking onto a flotilla of ships down the coast, Rommel raced his tanks south to trap them. When the enemy refused to surrender, the bridgehead was blasted with shell fire and Stuka dive-bombers strafed the beaches. By morning there was little fight in the troops huddling below the cliffs, and the French IX Corps and the British 51st (Highland) Division surrendered. Rommel's prisoners

An armoured column of Panzer 38T tanks moves up towards burning Soviet positions during the opening weeks of Operation Barbarossa, July 1941. Huge numbers of Soviet troops were left surrounded during the breakneck German advance.

included nine generals. One white-haired French general accused 48-year old Rommel of being a "far too fast, young man". His rant continued, "Sacre bleu! – The Ghost Division again. First in Belgium, then in Arras and on the Somme and now here, again and again our paths have crossed. We call you the Ghost Division."

Again Rommel pressed his panzers forward. With resistance crumbling, the 7th Panzer was clocking more than 160km (100 miles) a day. The finale of the campaign was the capture intact of the deep water port of Cherbourg. In a typical Rommel move, his panzers raced through the city's streets and caught the defenders unawares. By the end of 18 June, the 7th Division's haul of prisoners since the start of the campaign was approaching 97,000. Its own casualties ran to 200 dead and wounded, with 42 tanks lost. The ruthless advance of the Ghost Division epitomized the new German way of warfare. Its officers and soldiers proved expert practitioners at Blitzkrieg. The pedestrian Belgian, British and French armies just did not know what had hit them.

The 7th Panzer spent the summer and autumn of 1940 preparing for Operation Sea Lion – Hitler's proposed invasion of England. By the end of the year, however, the Führer had given up the idea of storming Great Britain's Channel moat and turned his attention towards his racial enemies – the Russians. For the invasion of the Soviet Union, the

7th Panzer Division was assigned to Hermann Hoth's 3rd Panzer Group. Rommel, however, did not head east with his men. He was ordered to Libya in February 1941 to command the Afrika Korps.

Operation Barbarossa kicked off in the early hours of 22 June 1941, with the 7th Panzer in the lead. This was very different to France. The Soviet Union was a vast country, with few metalled roads, bridges or other communications infrastructure. The Blitzkrieg quickly broke open the Soviet frontline, freeing the 7th Panzer to race into the interior of Stalin's empire. Small groups of Soviets put up sporadic resistance, but their command structure collapsed as German columns overran headquarters and cut telephone lines. Soon, thousands of leaderless Russians were trapped in huge pockets. 7th Panzer led the northern pincer that trapped 300,000 Soviets in the Smolensk Pocket in the middle of July. It took several months to clear up this pocket and an even bigger one at Kiev in the Ukraine. The 7th Panzer was then unleashed to continue the advance on Moscow, closing the pincers around another pocket at Vyasma, trapping some 600,000 Soviet troops. Rather than surrender, the Soviets put up ferocious resistance, rushing the German lines in human-wave charges. It took more than a month of hard fighting to subdue the resistance, by which time the weather had turned against the Germans. Heavy autumn rains transformed Russia into a quagmire. The Blitzkrieg was stalled.

THE 7TH HOLDS FAST AGAINST THE RED ARMY

By 19 November 1941, the temperature had dropped and the ground was frozen hard enough for the panzers to advance again. Operation Typhoon had the objective of seizing Moscow. 7th Panzer got to within 48km (30 miles) of Moscow before Russian resistance halted the advance. Huge snow drifts and freezing temperatures now shrouded the Eastern Front. Beleaguered groups of German soldiers found themselves on the receiving end of Soviet human-wave attacks, and slowly the Germans began to pull back. Units like the 7th Panzer formed defensive "hedgehogs" to ride out the storm. Only the leadership of determined commanders stopped the retreat becoming a route. The Soviets had held the German offensive, but failed to break open the German front. For the next five months the depleted 7th Panzer, commanded by General Hans Freiherr von Funck, was locked in a series of bloody defensive battles. In almost a year of fighting in Russia the division lost some 2000 men dead, 5600 wounded, 300 captured and over 1000 sick. Not surprisingly, the remnants of the division were relieved when they were pulled back to refit in France. The division received new up-gunned and up-armoured Panzer IV tanks, SdKfz 251 armoured halftracks, StuG III assault guns, Marder III self-propelled anti-tank guns and Wespe 105mm self-propelled howitzers. This new equipment meant it could pack a far more powerful punch to take on the newest Soviet T-34 tanks that had appeared in late 1941.

After the German Sixth Army was surrounded at Stalingrad in November 1942, Hitler ordered his panzer reserves to the Eastern Front to free the trapped 230,000 men. This time the 7th Panzer was prepared for the Russian winter, with special boots, quilted uniforms, and lubricants that kept its tanks and vehicles going in sub-zero temperatures. It took weeks for the trains carrying the 7th Panzer to reach the front in the Donets basin. Once in action, the division found itself being swept aside as the Soviets advanced westwards towards the Ukraine. Commanding the Wehrmacht's Army Group South was Germany's top general, Field Marshal Erich von Manstein, who was determined to turn the tables on the Soviets. He managed to husband his panzer divisions for a massive counterstroke to send the Soviets reeling back when they outran their supply lines. Veteran units such as 7th Panzer, by staging a series of deliberate withdrawal actions, succeeded in breaking contact with the Soviets but still kept their combat strength intact.

MANSTEIN'S COUNTERATTACK

By the middle of February 1943, the Soviet advance had run out of steam and von Manstein unleashed his armoured reserves. 7th Panzer prowled across the frozen Russian steppe, ambushing isolated groups of Soviet troops who were trying to flee for their lives. Stuka dive-bombers roamed ahead of the panzers, further adding to the chaos in the Red Army's ranks. It was like the old days for the 7th Panzer's troops, as they raced forward bypassing any resistance to maintain the momentum of the advance. The Soviets turned to fight south of Isyum and the 7th Panzer's tanks fought a brisk long-range engagement with dug-in Russian tanks and anti-tank guns, until the Panzer IVs silenced any resistance with their 75mm main armament. This battle broke the back of Soviet resistance south of the River Donets and vindicated von Manstein's strategy of mobile defence.

Hitler mustered his forces for another offensive on the Eastern Front in the summer of 1943, but 7th Panzer was set to play a secondary role in this attack as part of III Panzer Corps. Advancing on the southern wing of the German offensive, 7th Panzer acted as flank guard for II SS Panzer Corps during the Battle of Prokhorovka. During August, the division was engulfed in the huge Soviet offensive that drove the Germans from Kharkov. The German frontline collapsed and thousands of Soviet tanks surged westwards. Von Manstein called on his now seriously understrength panzer divisions to try to stem the tide. Major-General Hasso von Manteuffel was appointed divisional commander at the height of these battles, and was soon to be 7th Panzer's most famous leader after Rommel.

With less than 40 operational tanks 7th Panzer was sent into combat near Achtyrka, but after a swirling close-quarter battle, was able to link up with SS panzers advancing from the south and seal the front. The respite was only temporary, and soon a retreat was ordered to the Dnieper.

The dynamic von Manteuffel led 7th Panzer to its last major battle-field success in November 1943, as part of the German counteroffensive that regained Zhitomir. Four panzer divisions caught Soviet troops west of Kiev by surprise and pushed them back with heavy losses. 7th Panzer made a daring attack that surrounded and then cleared Zhitomir of resistance, before quickly resuming the offensive with a detachment of Tiger I heavy tanks. The next phase of the offensive called for 7th Panzer to advance at night along forest tracks to outflank the Soviets. With von Manteuffel at its head, the division successfully manoeuvred along frozen forest routes without any vehicles skidding off. His division then appeared out of the forests at Malini, deep in the Russian rear, causing immense panic in the Soviet ranks. The three other panzer divisions then struck and sent tens of thousands of Soviets fleeing for their lives. Regrouped and rearmed, 7th Panzer then formed one wing of a pincer move to trap three Soviet tanks corps massed on the German flank. 7th Panzer and the Waffen-SS *Leibstandarte* Division managed to close the ring around the Soviets, but they lacked the strength to completely subdue resistance.

The success around Zhitomir was short-lived. A new Soviet offensive south of Kiev broke just before Christmas 1943, and the whole of

A company of 7th Panzer's Panzer III Ausf Ms in Russia, summer of 1942 or 1943. The Ausf M came into service in early 1942 and carried the long 50mm KwK39 L/60 gun. This was inadequate against the new Soviet T-34 tank, which is probably why these Panzer IIIs carry extra tracks and additional sheet armour.

von Manstein's army group was thrown on the defensive. 7th Panzer found itself having to fight a series of bitter battles in terrible winter weather. Von Manteuffel's brief tour of command come to an end in January 1944, when a grateful Führer promoted him to lieutenant-general and gave him command of the elite *Grossdeutschland* Division. Soviet hammer blows hit von Manstein's command in rapid succession during the first three months of 1944, until they managed to surround the whole of the First Panzer Army, including the remnants of 7th Panzer, at Kamenets-Podolsk. It took two weeks for the "moving pocket" of trapped Germans to dodge past the Soviet entrapment.

After a quiet summer refitting the 7th Panzer was called to help restore the 320km (200-mile) breach created by the latest Soviet offensive. The division was rushed to the Courland region in August, where it was cut to pieces in the space of three months. By December, the remnants of the division were trapped in the bombed-out city of Memel, on the Baltic Sea. In a desperate evacuation, the exhausted survivors were loaded on German Navy ships for the journey to safety in East Prussia. Until January 1945, the division battled to hold the front south of Königsberg, when a massive Soviet offensive cleared German troops from Poland and trapped hundreds of thousands in East Prussia. In grim fighting, the German troops fought tenaciously but were relentlessly ground down by overwhelming odds. By early April 1945, 7th

The 7th Panzer Division seemed to attract some of the best divisional commanders the army had to offer. In 1940 Rommel had led it across France; in 1943 General Hasso von Manteuffel (centre) was to command it during some of the last great panzer battles on the Eastern Front.

Panzer was trapped on the Hela peninsula, north of Danzig, being swept by hellish shell fire as German ships tried to evacuate the increasingly desperate troops on the exposed beaches.

The few thousand survivors of the division were landed on the German Baltic coast, just as the Soviet offensive to capture Berlin got under way. Unable to contribute much to the final battle to defend the Third Reich, 7th Panzer was soon heading west in the hope of surrendering to the British or Americans rather than the vengeful Soviets. The division's surviving troops managed to surrender to the British at Schwerin on 3 May 1945.

In the five and a half years of its existence, the 7th Panzer Division epitomized Hitler's elite armoured force. Its advance across France saw the German Blitzkrieg drive all before it, with 7th Panzer in the vanguard blazing a trail that few other Wehrmacht units could match. The division was then committed to action on the Eastern Front for the remainder of the war, where it fought doggedly to hold back the Red Army's relentless advance. Charismatic leaders, like Rommel and von Manteuffel, led 7th Panzer to some of its most famous victories, while the division's highly professional command staff, regimental and battalion commanders ensured it always acquitted itself well. Divisions like the 7th Panzer were the backbone of Hitler's army in attack and defence. The 7th Panzer Division has since entered military legend as one of the world's premier armoured units.

The 7th Panzer Division, along with most of the First Panzer Army, was surrounded in January 1944 when the 1st and 2nd Ukrainian Fronts broke through a German salient during the Soviet winter offensive. Only General von Manstein's efforts saved it from destruction. These are Soviet T-34s carrying infantry.

7th Airborne – Student's Paras

Hitler was quick to embrace the idea of delivering troops into battle by parachute – it appealed to his vision of making the German armed forces modern and innovative, and also as a way to avoid the trench stalemate of World War I. By the mid-1930s, great advances were being made in the development of aircraft, so it was not surprising that there was great interest in military circles in using these machines to deliver elite fighting troops deep behind enemy lines.

A paratrooper takes part in a training exercise at the side door of a (grounded) Ju 52 transport, about 1939. He wears rubber knee pads used in training and a first-pattern jump smock. His helmet is an adaptation from the M1935 with cut down rim and "Y" leather chin-strap.

The first ever military parachute drop was made by a handful of Italian soldiers in 1927, but the first nation to fully explore the potential of this new form of warfare was the Soviet Union. In 1934, the Soviets conducted their first airborne exercises and even parachuted a tank. Soon the Red Army staged huge showcase manoeuvres near Moscow involving the dropping of more than 5000 paratroopers in front of foreign military attaches. They also began building gliders to deliver troops, vehicles and heavy equipment silently behind enemy lines.

When word of the Soviet developments reached Hermann Goering, head of the newly formed German Air Force, the Luftwaffe, he decided that Germany also needed paratroopers if it was not to let the Red Army gain an advantage over the Third Reich. Goering saw this as way to gain favour with his Führer and get one step ahead of the Army High Command. Goering wanted to convince Hitler that the Luftwaffe was following the Nazi Party's revolutionary path.

General Kurt Student (left, in peaked cap) organized the first German parachute division in the late 1930s and was in personal command during the Fallschirmjägers' first great victories at the Eben-Emael fortress and Crete. By 1942, however, he was forced to accede to Hitler's demand that his paratroopers be used as line infantry.

The Luftwaffe Regiment *Goering*, an airfield guard unit, was ordered to be redesignated as the new Fallschirmjägers (Paratroopers). The only problem was that no one in the unit knew how to use a parachute. Luftwaffe parachute instructors were drafted in, and soon the unit was gaining experience and a reputation for being a tough outfit that was backed by powerful people in the new Nazi regime. Recruits flocked to the new Fallschirmjägers, who were put through an incessant regime of jump and combat training. Major-General Kurt Student, a former World War I fighter pilot, was transferred to command the newly formed 7th Fallschirm or Parachute Division. Student was to be the father of the German airborne forces. He was a determined and cunning commander, as well as an able administrator and strategic thinker. From the start, he instilled his men with an aggressive "paratroop spirit". While no one doubted the bravery of the 48-year-old general, Student himself never actually qualified as a paratrooper.

Firstly, Student was able to win a bureaucratic battle with the German Army High Command to gain control of all the country's parachute forces, with the result that the army's own paratroop battalion was transferred to the Luftwaffe. Student, however, failed to get full control of the army's 22nd Air Landing Division; though this elite unit of infantrymen trained to fly into action on Junkers Ju 52 transport aircraft would work closely with Student's paratroopers in the future. Germany's first parachute general was also able to persuade the high command that his division should be used en masse to seize strategic objectives ahead of advancing panzer columns, rather than be frittered away in small sabotage missions behind enemy lines. Student's division was intended to be a potent strategic strike force.

Germany's airborne forces enjoyed one advantage not enjoyed by the airborne arms of other countries – they were part of the air force. This meant that both paratroops, air transport and strike aircraft could be employed as a single integrated force, and there were none of the inter-service disputes that dogged the development of the combined air-land operations in the British and American armed forces.

The Ju 52 was to be the workhorse of German parachute drops throughout World War II. Originally developed as a civilian transport for Lufthansa, and making its maiden flight in 1932, the three-engined Ju 52 was soon pressed into service by the newly formed Luftwaffe in the mid-1930s as both a military transport and an improvised bomber. While its distinctive ribbed metal fuselage and radial engines gave the Ju 52 an antiquated appearance, it was in fact a rugged and dependable aircraft. Its combat load of 18 paratroops could be carried some 1280km (800 miles) at 264kph (165mph). The aircraft's undercarriage was particularly robust, and meant it could be used to land troops on dirt airstrips, roads or any stretch of flat ground. In 1936, during the Spanish Civil War, Ju 52s were sent to help General Franco's fascists,

The Junkers Ju 52 was the primary transport aircraft of the Fallschirmjäger during their airborne assaults of 1940–41 – over 490 were used in the invasion of Crete alone. However, the Ju 52 was slow and as the war progressed suffered dreadfully high losses; by April 1945 only eight aircraft were left operational.

and one of their most important contributions was flying 10,000 of the general's troops from Africa to Spain at the outbreak of the conflict. Just under 5000 Ju 52s would be built in Germany before the end of the World War II, with the Ju 52/3m being the main version.

As well as transport aircraft, Luftwaffe commanders also recognized the military potential of gliders, and in 1937 authorized the mass production of the DFS 230. This could deliver eight fully armed soldiers silently into the heart of enemy territory, along with a significant amount of equipment. A single DFS 230 could be towed by a Ju 52 – also filled with paratroops – and then released close to the target, at which point the glider's own pilot took over. Gliders were envisaged as a first-strike weapon that could be launched into action even before paratroopers had landed. Their silent approach meant they gave the Germans the element of surprise, a crucial advantage in their aggressive airborne strategy. Once a bridgehead had been seized by glider and parachute-delivered assault troops, it was intended that cargo-carrying gliders would then be sent in to resupply them with ammunition and heavy equipment. These resupply gliders were still in development in 1940 and 1941, but they eventually came into production as the famous Gotha Go 242, which could carry a scout car or light howitzer, and the massive Messerschmitt Me 321, which could carry a tank. These two gliders were later fitted with engines to become powered transport aircraft.

At first the new German parachute force had to rely on the army for weapons and equipment, but soon it started generating requirements for the specialist items needed by airborne assault troops. The main need was to be able to fight and survive behind enemy lines with maximum firepower and minimum logistical back-up. Camouflage jump smocks and jump boots were provided. The traditional German steel helmet was adapted into padded parachute helmets that had a special

The Gotha Go 242 transport glider entered service in 1942, and was organized initially into six squadrons deployed to the Mediterranean and North Africa. Its usual towing aircraft was the He 111 bomber.

chin-strap to hold it firm and lacked the back rim, which could be potentially fatal during a rough landing. Special cloth bandoliers to carry extra ammunition were also developed.

Cargo containers that could be carried under the Ju 52 and dropped as the aircraft's paratroopers were jumping were mass produced, as a means of ensuring heavy MG 34 machine guns and ammunition were available immediately at the drop zone.

A project to develop one of the world's first assault rifles was also launched. This was to provide machine-gun rates of automatic fire-power, in a weapon that weighed little more than a conventional rifle. The result was the Fallschirmjägergewehr 42 and it entered service in 1942. It boasted a revolutionary gas-operated mechanism, which could fire from a closed bolt position for single-shot fire, and from an open bolt for automatic fire. This was to be the model for postwar assault rifles, such as the famous Kalashnikov AK-47.

The newly formed 7th Parachute Division sat out the invasion of Poland in the autumn of 1939 because Hitler wanted to save it for his attack on the West. It was crucial that the unique capabilities of this new force remained secret until absolutely necessary. Meanwhile, General Student spent time training and bringing his division up to strength for Operation Yellow, the invasion of France and the Low Countries. A special detachment of combat engineers or pioneers were earmarked to spearhead the assault on Belgium's frontier fortifications.

In April 1940, Hitler struck first against neutral Denmark and Norway. Three company sized parachute drops were made to help seize strategic Norwegian airfields. Follow-up waves of Ju 52s then landed infantrymen crammed inside. As the campaign reached its successful climax in early May, Hitler gave the go-ahead for Operation Yellow.

Early in 1941, the Me 321 heavy glider underwent a redesign into a powered transport aircraft. The result was the Me 323 *Gigant* (Giant), which entered service in November 1942 supplying the Afrika Korps out of Sicily. Production ceased in April 1944, after only 198 had been built.

The success of the German airborne attack on the Belgian fortress of Eben-Emael on 10 May 1940, was vital to secure the crossings of the Meuse and the Albert Canal. Student's plan was to take this "impregnable" fortress with a revolutionary coup-de-main assault on the roof of the fortress itself using glider-borne infantry.

Central to the German plan was the invasion of Belgium and Holland. It was hoped the British and French would send the bulk of their forces to these states to confront the invading German armies. Once they were committed, the Allies would be vulnerable to a panzer thrust through the thinly defended Ardennes region of southern Belgium. Student's new paratroops and the army's air landing division were to spearhead the assault on the Low Countries, which although being neutral, had built up impressive frontier defences to defeat any German invasion. These centred on securing or blowing a series of key bridges across the canals and rivers that would be vital to any invader. This resulted in the Germans dubbing their target "Fortress Holland", because the numerous water obstacles effectively became moats.

The first objective to be secured was the Belgium fort at Eben-Emael, near Liège, which dominated key bridges over the Albert Canal. They had to be captured to open the road for the panzers to move across the German frontier. For six months an 85-strong "assault" detachment drawn from the 1st Parachute Regiment and the 7th Parachute Division's pioneer battalion had been training for this mission. It was to use 11 DFS 230 gliders to land on the roof of the fort at dawn on 10 May 1940, and then disable its massive gun turrets with hollow-charge explosives before the defenders had time to realize what was happening. In conditions of great secrecy the force was trained and prepared. When the codeword was given, the gliders were moved in civilian furniture vans to the forward airfield to ensure operational security was not compromised.

In a light morning mist the gliders descended on their target and landed virtually unopposed. Some anti-aircraft guns opened fire, but the Belgian defenders had no idea what was about to happen. In the space of 10 minutes the assault troops captured or destroyed nine machine-gun bunkers. Then the pioneers moved to take out the huge metal rotating gun turrets with the hollow charges. These cut through the armour plate with ease and the 120mm gun barrels were then rendered useless by having charges detonated in their muzzles.

Belgian resistance was timid and ill-coordinated. The defenders cowered in the underground tunnels beneath the fort and did not dare come out to try to sweep the lightly armed Germans from the flat and exposed roof. By the time Belgian artillery opened fire and patrols started to probe the pioneers' positions, it was too late.

During the afternoon, the pioneers went on the offensive, dropping demolition charges down into the tunnels and galleries under the fort to further terrorize its defenders. Early on the morning of 11 May, a German relief column pushed across the Albert Canal. The remnants of the fort's 750-strong garrison surrendered. On the German side six pioneers had been killed and 15 wounded. The Allies had little idea what had happened, and for many years stories were circulated that

The German invasion of Holland began at dawn on 10 May 1940 with a series of parachute drops aimed at securing crossings of the Rhine, Maas and Lek Rivers. Other paratroops landed near Rotterdam's Waalhaven airport and The Hague.

Right: The airborne invasion of Crete. Operation Mercury was undertaken by XI Airborne Corps under General Student. Initial landings by elements of the 7th Airborne Division took place at four north coast towns on 20 May 1941.

the Germans had tunnelled into the fort. Surprise was total. The front door to Belgium had been opened for the 9th Panzer Division.

As the action was unfolding at Eben-Emael, the 7th Parachute Division was spearheading Student's ambitious plan to seize the gateways to "Fortress Holland". Three strong parachute detachments were already landing around the bridges over the Rhine, Maas and Lek Rivers south of Rotterdam. Farther north, other paratroops were landing around The Hague in an attempt to seize the Dutch government and Royal Family. Stuka dive-bombers had been at work softening up the Dutch defences ahead of the paratroopers. After the waves of Ju 52s had delivered their troops, the transport aircraft turned for their home bases to collect men of the 22nd Air Landing Division, who were to reinforce the paratroopers' bridgeheads.

Around Rotterdam, Student's attack went well. The paratroopers took the defenders by surprise and quickly seized the key bridges. Soon the Dutch recovered their poise and mounted vigorous counterattacks. A Dutch Navy cruiser even joined the battle, bombarding the German bridgehead until Stukas drove it off. Desperate fighting took place until the panzers arrived to relieve them. Controversy, however, surrounded an air strike called by Student on Rotterdam. The Dutch commander agreed to a truce, but the message calling off the bombing raid failed to get through to the aircraft, causing large-scale loss of life amongst the city's civilian population. In the subsequent confusion, Student was shot accidentally by a Waffen-SS sniper and severely wounded.

Farther north, the battle did not progress as planned. The initial landings were contained by the Dutch and their Royal Family and government managed to escape the coup de main. Many of the paratroopers were dropped in the wrong places, so when the Ju 52s carrying the air landing troops approached the three airfields around The Hague they found the Dutch defenders fully alerted. Dozens of Ju 52s were shot-up and hundreds of German troops killed. A counterattack by three Dutch divisions drove the paratroops and air landing troops from their drop zones around the airfields, preventing reinforcement and resupply. The air landing division's commander, General Count Hans von Sponeck, was badly wounded in the fighting as his troops formed defensive "hedge-hogs" to hold on until they were finally relieved several days later.

In the wake of the successful invasion of "Fortress Holland", General Student was ordered to take command of the new XI Airborne Corps, which incorporated both the 7th and 22nd Divisions, for the proposed invasion of England, Operation Sea Lion. When Hitler cancelled this he turned his attention eastwards, but a pro-British coup in Yugoslavia in April 1941 forced him to divert troops to the Balkans to secure his southern flank. A panzer Blitzkrieg smashed Yugoslavia and then pushed a British expeditionary force back into Greece. Student's paratroopers were given the job of seizing the Corinth Canal bridge to trap thousands

After Crete and a period on the Eastern Front, elements of the parachute corps were reorganized into the 1st Parachute Division and sent to the Mediterranean as a strategic reserve. On 9 November 1942 they were flown into Tunisia from Sicily, and deployed there as elite infantry units (below).

By the end of 1942 the Fallschirmjäger had lost their airborne role and were used increasingly as line infantry. This did nothing to undermine their fighting spirit – a fact demonstrated in Italy during the defence of Monte Cassino by the 1st Parachute Division in early 1944.

of retreating British and Greek troops. Two battalions of paratroops successfully landed on either end of the bridge and stormed the bunkers containing the triggers for the demolition charges. In the confusion, sniper fire set the charges off. The bridge was blown sky-high, killing and wounding scores of Germans.

By late April the British had pulled back their troops to the island of Crete, 192km (120 miles) south of Athens. Hitler was worried that the British would turn the island into a bomber base to threaten his strategic oil wells in Romania. He was determined to seize the island before the start of Operation Barbarossa, the invasion of the Soviet Union, and gave the task to Student's XI Airborne Corps. Operation Mercury was to be the first ever invasion conducted principally by air. Student had his 7th Division and the 5th Mountain Division, which replaced the 22nd Division in the air landing role, for the operation. His plan envisaged landing 10,000 men by parachute, 5000 in transport aircraft while 7000 more were to be landed by sea. More than 500 Ju 52s and 80 gliders were concentrated for the attack.

Holding the island were some 30,000 British, Australian and New Zealand troops, 11,000 Greek soldiers as well as tens of thousands of armed Cretan civilians. New Zealand General B.C. Freyberg's forces lacked armour, artillery and ammunition, and his handful of fighters were totally outclassed by the Luftwaffe, which had 280 bombers, 150 dive-bombers, 180 fighters and 40 photographic reconnaissance aircraft.

After a major effort by the Luftwaffe to soften up the defences, the first parachute landings by 3000 Germans took place on the morning of

20 May. Although poorly equipped, Freyberg's troops put up fanatical resistance. They had been waiting for parachute landings, and local commanders quickly ordered determined counterattacks to prevent the German paratroops securing a foothold. Hundreds of Fallschirmjäger were machine-gunned as they drifted to earth. Local civilians joined in this "turkey shoot" and took axes and shovels to paratroopers tangled in olive trees. Those that survived this ordeal soon found themselves pinned down in small enclaves on the edges of Crete's four airfields at Maleme, Canea, Retimo and Heraklion. Communications broke down so follow-up waves of paratroops were dropped on the same zones and suffered equally heavy casualties. By the end of day, Canea, Retimo and Heraklion remained firmly in British hands, with the German attackers driven off. Only at Maleme did Student's forces have any prospect of achieving their objective. Roving Luftwaffe patrols kept the British pinned down during daylight hours, which was instrumental in preventing Freyberg from mopping up the German pockets.

Fallschirmjägers and New Zealand infantrymen fought hand-to-hand on a key hill that dominated Maleme airfield all through the night of 20/21 May. In the confused fighting the New Zealand commander ordered his men to pull back. The Germans then capitalized on the mistake, and by early the following morning a Ju 52 made a daredevil landing at Maleme to deliver the first reinforcements. By the time the pilot had returned safely, the base was in German hands. Student now ordered everything to be concentrated on expanding this tenuous toe-

It took five months and four major attacks before Allied divisions finally dislodged the paratroopers from Monte Cassino on 17 May 1944. The weapon here is the FG 42 (first model); a semi/fully automatic assault rifle specially developed for airborne forces, but produced in only limited numbers.

The Fallschirmjäger played a leading role during the battles to halt the Allied invasion of Europe in 1944. II Parachute Corps' defence around St Lô, Normandy, in July, and its deployment in the Ardennes Offensive the following December – seen here – secured the paras' reputation as some of Germany's finest soldiers.

hold on Crete. During the day, hundreds of Ju 52s and gliders packed with paratroops and mountain soldiers landed at Maleme. Scores of Ju 52s were damaged or shot down, but Student's gamble had paid off. When Freyberg finally launched a brigade-sized counterattack during the night it was too late. The German line held. A German naval flotilla bringing in heavy supplies, artillery and reinforcements was intercepted by the Royal Navy and scattered. Student's men would have to rely on air support alone to support their drive to secure the rest of the island.

In three frantic days, Student's Ju 52 crews shuttled back and forth to Maleme until he was ready to launch his offensive. It took four days of hard fighting for the Fallschirmjägers and mountain troops to sweep along the north coast of Crete to capture Suda Bay naval base and link up with many of the scattered pockets of paratroopers. With no artillery, the Germans relied on Stuka dive-bombers to blast open the Allied lines. Under relentless pressure and with no means to stop the German build-up, Freyberg ordered Crete abandoned on 28 May. His troops beat a desperate retreat through the island's high mountains to the south coast. The Royal Navy managed to lift just over 15,000 men off the beaches, but some 2000 sailors died when 9 ships were sunk and 15 damaged by the Luftwaffe.

Student and his men had achieved a brilliant feat of arms that was a notable military first – capturing an enemy held island by air. A heavy price was paid in blood and materiel for this victory. Just over 3250 Germans died and a similar number were wounded. Some 200 Ju 52s were destroyed or badly damaged. The 7th Parachute Division was decimated and would be out of action for several months.

The high cost of Operation Mercury meant that Hitler was reluctant to sanction airborne attacks on Malta and Gibraltar. Over the next 18 months almost every element of Student's corps was sent to the Russian Front to fight as line infantry, where they suffered horrendous casualties. It was not until the end of 1942 that new orders were issued to reform a parachute-capable division, now designated the 1st Parachute Division, in southern France, as a strategic reserve for the Mediterranean theatre. Elements of the division were airlifted to Tunisia to help build up the German defensive line against Allied troops advancing westward from Morocco and Algeria.

When Allied troops landed in Italy in July 1943, Germany's paratroops would get the chance to go into battle against the British Army's Parachute Regiment. The Red Berets seized a key bridge south of Catania in the opening hours of the invasion. In response the German 3rd Parachute Regiment was ordered to drop on the bridge to retake it. After a series of air raids, the Germans landed on either side of the bridge and swiftly overwhelmed the 200-strong British garrison. They held the bridge for only a few hours before a British armoured brigade was sent to finish off the Germans. In savage hand-to-hand fighting the German paratroops were driven back, but not before they inflicted 500 casualties on the British. Some 300 Germans lay dead and 160 were captured.

LAST ACTIONS

Another parachute drop was made during the operation to recapture the Greek island of Leros on November 1943, but the German airborne force was now a mere shadow of itself. Allied air supremacy meant that the prospect of large-scale parachute drops in daylight were now impossible. SS paratroopers were used in a surprise attack on the headquarters of the Yugoslav partisan leader Tito in 1944, with some success. The remains of the Luftwaffe's paratroopers now had to fight out the war as line infantry. Eventually Goering formed 10 more parachute divisions. They were little more than glorified infantry and were not jump-trained, but still retained plenty of the old Fallschirmjäger spirit. The tenacious defence of the Monte Cassino positions in Italy during 1944 by the 1st Parachute Division has entered military legend. In the run-up to the German Ardennes Offensive in December 1944, the Luftwaffe was ordered to form a parachute battalion by drafting surviving jump-trained personnel from every corner of the now diminished Reich. The operation was a fiasco. Flying at night in a blizzard, the Ju 52s dropped the paratroops over a wide area, and only 100 or so men were able to muster on the drop zone. They could do little more than escape and evade back to German lines in small groups.

In six years of war, Hitler's paratroopers had blazed a trail to prove a new way of warfare. Although the heavy losses on Crete made Hitler cautious about further airborne operations, the Allies took up the idea. In September they launched Operation Market Garden to drop an "airborne carpet" of paratroops and glider-borne infantry to seize the Rhine bridges in Holland, and open the way for Allied armour to advance into the heart of Germany. It was almost a repeat of Student's invasion plan of 1940, though far less successful.

Leibstandarte Adolf Hitler

Born out of a group of street brawlers in the 1920s whose job was to protect leading Nazi figures from political violence, Adolf Hitler's bodyguard grew into one of the finest armoured divisions of World War II. Under the unique leadership of "Sepp" Dietrich, it helped save the Eastern Front from collapse in 1943 and 1944. Regarded as invincible by its Führer, its members ended the war bitter and disillusioned when Hitler finally turned on them.

An honour guard of the *Adolf Hitler* Standarte, 1933. The *Leibstandarte* originated in 1933 as a hand-picked group of 120 SS men who were to act as Hitler's personal armed bodyguard. They received the title *Leibstandarte-SS Adolf Hitler* from Hitler himself on 9 November 1933.

The first Waffen-SS unit to bear the name of the Führer of the Third Reich was the *Leibstandarte SS Adolf Hitler*. In the space of eight years it grew from a small band of bodyguards and political enforcers into a battle-hardened motorized infantry division. Over the next four years the *Leibstandarte* blazed a trail through western Europe, the Balkans and Russia. It became the Nazi elite unit par excellence, combining fanatical fighting spirit with political loyalty and superb tactical skill in the face of overwhelming odds.

Hitler's paranoid political philosophy was born in his street fighting days of the early 1920s. Germany was on the verge of revolution. Coup attempts were a regular occurrence as the country's fledgling democracy tried to cope with the aftermath of defeat in World War I. The Nazi Brown Shirts, or Sturm Abteilung (SA), were at the forefront of clashes with communists and the police of the Weimar Republic. When Hitler's so-called Beer Hall Putsch failed in November 1923, the future dictator became convinced that he needed a reliable elite paramilitary group at his disposal if he was ever to seize and hold power in Germany.

As Germany spiralled into economic depression, and mass unemployment took hold in the aftermath of the "Great Depression" of 1929, Hitler saw his chance. While participating in elections that brought him to the brink of power, Hitler also began mobilizing his paramilitary forces. Central to his strategy was a small shadowy group of just over 100 young men known as the Shutz Staffel (Protection Squad), or SS. Dressed in sinister black uniforms, the SS appeared to the uninitiated to be little more than Hitler's bodyguards. They were, in fact, the armed elite of the Nazi Party, loyal only to Hitler. The list of the membership of the first SS group reads like a who's who of the future Waffen-SS (Armed-SS). It was led by one Joseph "Sepp" Dietrich, who rose to command the *Leibstandarte SS Adolf* Hitler Division and ultimately the Sixth SS Panzer Army, which would contain six Waffen-SS panzer divisions in its final days in April 1945. Many of the famous wartime Waffen-SS divisional and regimental commanders were members of this first group, and the bond served them well through the war and beyond.

THE GROWTH OF THE SS

Once Hitler rose to the chancellorship of Germany in January 1933, he moved swiftly to consolidate his hold on power. One of his first acts was the violent elimination of the leadership of the SA in the famous "Night of the Long Knives". This saw the SS in the thick of the action, seizing scores of SA leaders and then executing them. Dietrich played a prominent part in this purge, overseeing the first extra-judicial killings under Hitler's regime. From this point on the nature of Germany changed. No longer was it a parliamentary democracy, governed by the rule of law. For the next 12 years it would be fascist dictatorship, with the SS acting as Hitler's ruthless killing machine.

In a matter of months, the SS grew into a form of parallel government, to ensure the Nazi Party could never be overthrown from within. The police, prison service, intelligence agencies and judiciary were all kept under close control by their SS counterparts. Soon the SS boasted hundreds of thousands of members, all working to ensure total obedience to the Führer's will.

Not surprisingly, Hitler viewed the Germany armed forces or Wehrmacht with great suspicion. They alone seemed to possess the wherewithal to remove the Nazi regime from power. The former "Bohemian corporal" had little time for the aristocratic professional officers corps of the Germany Army, who he blamed for Germany's defeat in World War I. Hitler immediately set about neutralizing the political power of the General Staff. He made every German soldier swear a personal oath of loyalty to him; troublesome senior commanders were removed after trumped-up sex scandals (such as Field Marshal Werner von

Blomberg) and others were bought off with gifts of huge estates. Still Hitler was worried. So he decided to expand his elite bodyguard force into the Nazi Party's own mini-army. It would be the only official armed force in Germany, with an official mandate to take armed action within the borders of the new Third Reich. The Wehrmacht would be limited to fighting foreign wars. Thus the Waffen-SS was born.

It was in these early days that the Waffen-SS developed its unique ethos. Recruits were screened for racial purity. They had to be able to trace their "bloodline" back through several generations to prove they had no Jewish relatives. Physical imperfections, such as fillings or poor eyesight, also counted against membership of the Waffen-SS.

The prominent public role of the first Waffen-SS unit, the *Leibstandarte*, in guarding Hitler and public buildings in Berlin quickly led to them being dubbed the "Asphalt Soldiers" by the Wehrmacht. They were only fit for parades, claimed the cynics. Behind the scenes, Hitler and the head of the overall SS organization, Heinrich Himmler, set in train a series of moves to turn the Waffen-SS into an elite military formation.

A number of professional staff officers, such as Paul Hausser and Willi Bittrich, were recruited to set up junior officer and noncommissioned officer schools, run staff officer courses and organize logistics. These men ensured that professional military discipline and standards endured in the ranks of the Waffen-SS, rather than the political cronyism that was rampant in other parts of Hitler's Nazi empire.

The first commander of the *Leibstandarte*, Joseph "Sepp" Dietrich, seen here after the campaign in France in 1940. Dietrich's personal friendship with Hitler ensured the growth and independence of the *Leibstandarte*. The unit became motorized in 1934, years before most of the army.

The first Waffen-SS units were termed standarten and they were merely lightly equipped infantry units. Hitler, however, was determined to ensure his Waffen-SS had the best weapons and equipment. Soon heavy machine guns, mortars, light artillery and armoured cars were being delivered to Waffen-SS depots.

By the late 1930s the Waffen-SS standarten had grown into superbly equipped motorized infantry regiments. They bore the titles, including *Leibstandarte* and *Totenkopf*, that would soon be household names during World War II.

As war approached, Hitler ordered the Waffen-SS standarten to be grouped together in a single division, the SS-VT. It was included in the war planning for the invasion of Poland, where Hitler hoped it would cover itself in glory against a nation of people who he considered racially subhuman, or "untermenschen".

The combat debut of the Waffen-SS occurred during the September 1939 invasion of Poland, where the SS-VT Division was assigned to the Wehrmacht's Army Group South. The Poles put up patchy resistance and the SS-VT was hardly taxed, although Hitler enthused about his elite unit's performance.

The following spring, the Waffen-SS standarten were expanded into fully fledged motorized infantry regiments, now boasting assault gun battalions equipped with StuG IIIs. Hitler's favourite regiment, the *Leibstandarte*, was assigned to support the panzer drive through Holland and Belgium. Here it clashed with British soldiers, and a detachment under the command of SS-Hauptsturmführer Wilhelm Mohnke massacred a squad of 80 captured British troops.

Again, Hitler was overjoyed at what he saw as the dazzling combat performance of his Waffen-SS troops and ordered yet another expansion of the force. This time there were to be four SS motorized divisions; the *Leibstandarte*, *Das Reich*, *Totenkopf* and *Wiking*. These four

A Waffen-SS MG 34 team on the Eastern Front, August 1941. SS units such as the *Leibstandarte* pioneered the use of camouflage uniforms, first adopting helmet covers during the campaign in France in 1940.

units were to be the core of the Waffen-SS for the duration of the war, and officers from them would find themselves in great demand as Hitler expanded his elite force into a fully functioning private army of some 35 divisions, to rival the Wehrmacht.

The performance of the *Leibstandarte* during the invasions of Yugoslavia and Greece in April 1941 created something of a stir in the Wehrmacht high command. Its tactical flair and efficiency impressed senior army commanders, who were now beginning to appreciate that the Waffen-SS were not just parade ground soldiers.

In the invasion of Russia in June 1941, the *Leibstandarte* numbered 10,796 men. The four Waffen-SS divisions were in the thick of the action, spearheading the dramatic Blitzkrieg advances deep behind Soviet lines. Hitler's declarations that the war on the Eastern Front was a racial crusade for *lebensraum*, or "living space", for the German people, was taken up with enthusiasm by the Waffen-

SS troops, who executed Soviet prisoners in large numbers and helped SS Einsatzgruppen murder squads hunt down and kill Jews. The *Leibstandarte* was attached to Army Group South for Operation Barbarossa and spearheaded the German advance through the Ukraine. In spite of capturing hundreds of thousands of Russians in huge pockets around Kiev, Soviet resistance stiffened as winter approached. In the depths of the Russian winter "Sepp" Dietrich's men fought a tenacious battle to hold the front around Rostov-on-Don.

Nazi arrogance had led Hitler to believe his armies could defeat the Russians by the autumn, with the result that there were no supplies of winter clothing or equipment for the German troops. Only the tenacious resistance of units such as the three Waffen-SS divisions, *Leibstandarte*, *Das Reich* and *Totenkopf*, held the German

Motorcycle sidecar combinations, such as this one from the *Leibstandarte*, formed part of a panzer division's reconnaissance units and worked alongside armoured cars and halftracks. By 1944 it was usual to have as many as 40 operational within a panzer battalion.

A Tiger I Ausf E of the *Leibstandarte* Division on the Normandy Front in 1944. The *Leibstandarte* was reorganized into a panzergrenadier division 1942, but to retain its armoured "punch" kept a full panzer regiment on-strength, including heavy tank battalions of Tigers.

front together, preventing a rout. By the spring, the Waffen-SS units were decimated but they had firmly established their fighting reputation. The Waffen-SS had entered Russia with 160,405 men. By mid-November it had suffered 36,517 killed, wounded or missing.

Hitler's suspicion of his generals was increased after the retreat from Moscow in December 1941, so he ordered the three Waffen-SS divisions to be pulled out of Russia and shipped to France to be rebuilt as so-called panzergrenadier divisions, although they were to have a full panzer regiment on-strength, effectively making them the equivalent of an army panzer division.

The divisions spent the summer and autumn of 1942 re-equipping and retraining for their new role under the command of the new SS Panzer Corps of Paul Hausser. The encirclement of the German Sixth Army at Stalingrad in November 1942 forced Hitler to order Hausser's new formation to southern Russia to relieve the 230,000 trapped men. Needless to say, the task was way beyond the capabilities of the Waffen-SS corps. It ended up being surrounded itself in the Ukrainian city of Kharkov, and only escaped when Hausser ignored Hitler's orders to fight to the last man. Dietrich was in the thick of the action as usual. When the cunning commander of Army Group South, Field Marshal Erich von Manstein, organized a devastating counterattack against the over-exposed Soviet tank columns, the *Leibstandarte* was in the first line of attack. Its Panzer

IVs and Tigers ripped into the Soviets, killing thousands of Russian troops and destroying hundreds of T-34 tanks.

Hausser and his troops redeemed themselves in the eyes of their Führer by leading the counteroffensive that retook Kharkov in March 1943 – it was the *Leibstandarte* which led the attack into the city.

Four months later, Hausser's corps spearheaded the German offensive at Kursk and found itself locked in the largest tank battle in military history. After over a week of heavy fighting the Soviet defences held, and the Germans were forced on the defensive along almost the entire Eastern Front. Again the *Leibstandarte* spearheaded the German advance and bore the brunt of the attack by the Soviet Fifth Guards Tank Army at Prokhorovka on 12 July. The Waffen-SS division, with only 70 tanks and assault guns, held off 800 Soviet tanks throughout that fateful day, claiming more than 200 destroyed.

The *Leibstandarte* was briefly sent to Italy to counter the Allied invasion in July 1943, but by November it was recalled to the East to help shore up a rapidly deteriorating situation. The division remained on the Eastern Front for the next four months, suffering horrendous losses as it tried to hold Army Group South's front together. The *Leibstandarte* led a counterattack against Kiev in November, but was thrown onto the defensive by a huge Soviet tank offensive in December. When 50,000 German troops were trapped in the Korsun-Cherkassy Pocket in February 1944, the *Leibstandarte* spearheaded the doomed rescue attempt. A few weeks later the division was itself trapped in the Kamenets-Poldolsk Pocket and only managed to escape after von Manstein disobeyed Hitler's orders to fight to the last man, ordering a "moving pocket" to be formed.

SS PANZER EXPANSION

Buoyed by the success of the SS at Kharkov and the failure of the army panzer divisions to relieve Stalingrad, Hitler decided on a major expansion of the Waffen-SS panzer force during the spring of 1943. A second panzer corps headquarters was to be formed, dubbed I *Leibstandarte* SS Panzer Corps, under the command of the Führer's old favourite, "Sepp" Dietrich. It was nominally to consist of the *Leibstandarte* Division and a newly formed division, to be recruited from the ranks of the Nazi youth movement, the Hitler Youth or Hitlerjugend. The *Leibstandarte* was to provide a cadre of experience officers and soldiers for the new corps headquarters and the new division. By the autumn of 1943 the new units were being formed in training depots in Belgium, although the *Leibstandarte* Division itself would not join them until the following spring when it was released from the Eastern Front.

In the autumn of 1943, a new designation system was introduced, with the panzergrenadier divisions officially renamed as panzer divisions; so for example, the premier Waffen-SS unit became the 1st SS Panzer Division *Leibstandarte SS Adolf Hitler*, or LSSAH for short.

The new Waffen-SS panzer units were initially slow to take shape, with new recruits and equipment arriving in dribs and drabs. As winter approached and it became clearer that the British and Americans would soon launch their invasion of France, the pace of training and equipping took on greater urgency. Soon new tanks, armoured half-tracks and other weapons were flowing to France.

Shattered by its experiences on the Eastern Front, the *Leibstandarte* was pulled back to France in the spring of 1944 to be rebuilt to spearhead Hitler's counter-invasion strategy. The half-starved and lice-infested remnants of the division were in no shape to do much beyond clean and repair their paltry stocks of weapons and vehicles.

Soon the Waffen-SS replacement and supply system kicked in. New soldiers and equipment started to arrive in quantities. Time was short, however, and the quality of the new recruits left a lot to be desired. Most were drafted youngsters or former Luftwaffe and Navy personnel. They were not of the same quality as the volunteers that had made their way into the ranks of the elite Waffen-SS divisions earlier in the war. The cadre of *Leibstandarte* veterans had to begin almost from scratch, teaching these new Waffen-SS basic soldiering skills, while at the same time indoctrinating them into their "divisional family".

By the late spring of 1944, the five Waffen-SS panzer and one panzergrenadier division earmarked to repulse the impending Allied invasion of France boasted some of the most powerful weapons in the German arsenal. The most common tank was the Panzer V or Panther. With its sloped armour, wide tracks and powerful 75mm cannon, it could out-shoot, out-manoeuvre and out-armour almost every Allied tank. The

A *Leibstandarte* panzergrenadier SdKfz 250 halftrack on the Eastern Front. This is the 250/3 radio communications variant, featuring the large frame antenna.

Panther could take out the most common Allied tank, the Sherman, at some 2000m (2188yd) range, whereas a Sherman had to close to within 500m (547yd) to stand a chance of penetrating the sloped side armour of the German monster. The lighter Panzer IV was more evenly matched with the Sherman, but its 75mm gun still gave it a considerable range advantage and it had armoured skirts to neutralize Allied hollow-charge bazookas or PIAT launchers. Both Panthers and Panzer IVs served in the panzer battalions of the Waffen-SS divisions.

The most feared German tank was the Tiger I, with its famous 88mm cannon. Its 100mm (4in) frontal armour was impenetrable to most Allied tank guns. The only thing that stood a chance of penetrating a Tiger's frontal armour was the British 17-pounder gun with its revolutionary discarding tungsten sabot round. The Tiger served in heavy tank companies attached to Waffen-SS panzergrenadier divisions during 1943, but were later formed into independent battalions. In the autumn of 1944, the Tiger II or King Tiger was introduced.

Waffen-SS units also boasted large numbers of Jagdpanzer IV, StuG III and Marder self-propelled guns. These were based on converted tank chassis, but lacked rotating turrets. Their heavy cannons were

Out of the mists of a Russian winter comes one of the *Leibstandarte*'s Panzer IVs. Despite the accalaim given to the Tigers and Panthers, the Panzer IV was the backbone of the panzer units, including those of the Waffen-SS. This is an Ausf G or H.

The commander of the SS Panzer Corps, General Paul Hausser. Organized at the end of 1942, the corps was one of the largest Waffen-SS formations assembled to that date and consisted of the *Leibstandarte*, *Das Reich* and *Totenkopf* Divisions.

mounted low in their hulls, making them easy to camouflage and ideal defensive weapons. The Jagdpanzer IV was based on a Panzer IV chassis. It had the same long-barrelled 75mm cannon as the Panther and thick, sloped armour. The StuG III was smaller, being based on the obsolete Panzer III, but it had a useful 75mm cannon. The Marder was a lightly armoured tank hunter, based on a Czech tank chassis and mounting the powerful captured Russian 76.2mm anti-tank gun.

At the heart of each Waffen-SS panzer division were two panzergrenadier regiments or mechanized infantry. Each one had an anti-tank company, either with Marders or towed PaK-40 anti-tank guns. Panzergrenadier companies were lavishly equipped with the shoulder-fired Panzerschreck anti-tank rocket launcher, which was copied from the American bazooka, or the "throw-away" one-shot Panzerfaust anti-tank weapon. These weapons turned every infantry squad into tank hunters.

One panzergrenadier battalion in each division was mounted in armoured SdKfz 251 halftracks, known as SPWs, to allow it to accompany the panzer battalion into close proximity with the enemy. The other five panzergrenadier battalions were carried in soft-skinned trucks. The divisional reconnaissance battalion also had armoured halftracks and Marders.

TACTICS

Their experiences in Russia had transformed the Waffen-SS panzer divisions into some of the most professional armoured formations the world had ever seen. Under experienced commanders, such as Hausser, Dietrich, Kurt "Panzer" Meyer and Joachim Peiper, the Waffen-SS panzer divisions were masters of their art.

Central to German armoured doctrine was the idea of the all-arms battlegroup (kampfgruppe). Unlike the situation in Allied armies, it was considered routine for Waffen-SS formations to quickly form battlegroups, combining tank, panzergrenadier, anti-tank, reconnaissance and artillery units under a single commander. There was no set size or shape for a battlegroup, which depended on the mission and the enemy being faced.

The close-knit Waffen-SS "family" made the formation and functioning of battlegroups even more effective than in Wehrmacht panzer units. Waffen-SS officers had all served with each other for several years, so they knew how their comrades operated and could easily become a member of their command staff. Conducting complex tactical manoeuvres, through brief verbal orders issued over the radio, time and again quickly formed Waffen-SS battle groups would save the day for the Germans. On the Allied side, formal and laborious "orders groups" were the norm, making it difficult for operations to be rapidly improvised.

Mission command was at the heart of German tactics. Commanders were given an objective to achieve and left to formulate a plan to achieve their command's intent. During defensive and offensive operations, German commanders would decide what was the schwerpunkt (point of man effort) and concentrate their resources to secure that objective. In the defensive battles in Normandy this usually resulted in the Germans trying to hold a key piece of high ground that could dominate a large area, allowing devastating artillery, mortar and tank fire to be brought to bear against the enemy. When the Waffen-SS moved to attack, the same principle was used but with the bulk of German offensive power being concentrated against the weakest point in the Allied line. Once success had been achieved, then overwhelming force was concentrated to reinforce that initial success.

The Waffen-SS had learnt on the Eastern Front that its tanks were true battle-winning weapons, both in the attack and defence, as long as they were concentrated and used en masse. A division's panzer regiment would only be committed to action if it could achieve decisive results. It was not to be wasted away in penny packets, holding ground or in limited attacks. The job of holding ground was to be left to the panzergrenadiers, supported by the anti-tank units and maybe the anti-aircraft battalion's 88mm flak guns operating in the direct fire role.

The *Leibstandarte* Division was still refitting and training at its Belgian bases when the Allies landed in Normandy on 6 June 1944.

The *Leibstandarte* (this is one of its anti-tank guns) arrived at the Allied invasion front in Normandy in July 1944 and was organized, along with the *Hitlerjugend* Division, into I SS Panzer Corps under its old commander, "Sepp" Dietrich.

Transport problems and equipment shortages meant the division was not able to enter the line alongside the other units of I SS Panzer Corps until mid-July. Its first major action was blunting the British advance east of Caen during Operation Goodwood, knocking out 400 Shermans of the Guards, 77th and 11th Armoured Divisions. After US troops broke through the western part of the German line in late-July, Hitler ordered his Waffen-SS panzers to counterattack at Mortain on 7 August and seal the breach. The effort was a lost cause even before the first panzer went into action. Allied fighter-bombers found the German columns as they moved across northern France, inflicting huge losses. Within days the Germans were in retreat eastwards, and then the jaws of the Allied pincers closed in on them. Around Falaise the whole of the German Army in Normandy, including the *Leibstandarte*, was trapped. Hausser and other Waffen-SS commanders in the pocket ordered their men to break out in defiance of their Führer's orders.

THE LAST BATTLE

After a headlong retreat across France, the Germans managed to form a new line on the Third Reich's western frontier. Hitler was not content to stay on the defensive, though. He ordered planning to start on a new offensive to drive the Allies from France. Under Operation Wacht am Rhein, refitted Waffen-SS panzer units, including the *Leibstandarte*, were to dash through the Ardennes region of Belgium to seize the post of Antwerp, trapping hundreds of thousands of Allied troops. It was audacious, but the troops were woefully ill-prepared for the operation.

The *Leibstandarte* had the dubious honour of leading the advance, with Joachim Peiper's armoured battlegroup being given the job of seizing the strategic bridges across the Meuse to open the way to Antwerp. Peiper's troops achieved infamy when they shot almost 100 US prisoners of war at Malmédy. A few days later, his column ran out of petrol and was trapped by US troops. The German offensive stalled, and by early January the *Leibstandarte* was back in Germany.

Hitler again ordered the rebuilding of his Waffen-SS divisions but this time his target was Hungary. He wanted to secure the country's oil wells and drive back Soviet troops that were besieging Budapest. The *Leibstandarte* enjoyed early success in Operation Spring Awakening in January 1945, before huge Soviet tank reserves forced it to retreat towards Vienna, which it reached in April. At the same time, Russian troops were opening their attack on Berlin and the Allies were across the Rhine. Germany was finished. In his Berlin bunker, Hitler was enraged by the retreat of the *Leibstandarte* and ordered his troops to remove their "Adolf Hitler" arm cuffs. This was the last straw for *Leibstandarte* veterans, such as Dietrich. They ordered their men to beat a retreat westwards, with the aim of surrendering to the Americans.

Two of the senior Waffen-SS commanders on the Normandy Front, 1944. "Sepp" Dietrich (left), head of I SS Panzer Corps, and General Fritz Witt, commander of the *Hitlerjugend*. Both men were former members of *Leibstandarte* Division.

The *Leibstandarte* Division never formally surrendered. It simply melted away when its commanders ordered their men to make their way back to their homes. Eventually the bulk of the *Leibstandarte* men were captured, however. After the war the Americans were determined to bring the men of the *Leibstandarte* to trial for their crimes at Malmédy. As a result, more than 70 were tried at the old SS concentration camp at Dachau and sentenced to long terms in prison. In the end, however, as the Cold War burst into life and the Soviet Union became the new enemy of the West, the Americans lost interest and eventually the *Leibstandarte* veterans were released. For men such as "Sepp" Dietrich, who had surrendered to the Americans rather than the Russian, it was a lucky escape.

In its brief existence, the *Leibstandarte* established a fearsome reputation on the battlefields of Europe. It was the elite unit against which other Nazi elite units judged themselves.

By the summer of 1944, the tank crews of the *Leibstandarte* began to be typified by their youth and strange mix of available uniforms.

Left: The *Leibstandarte* narrowly missed destruction in Normandy. Only the efforts of its senior commanders saved it from the Allied pincer attack of August and the threat of enemy fighter-bombers. These German tanks were not so lucky.

CHAPTER 4

U-Boats – Dönitz's Ship Killers

In six years of conflict, the German U-boats came to within an ace of winning the Battle of the Atlantic and forcing Great Britain to its knees. U-boat crews threw themselves into the fight with a vengeance, U-boat captains proved themselves to be skilled and fanatical opponents, and the "ace" U-boat commanders sent millions of tonnes of Allied of shipping to the bottom of the Atlantic. Few captains or their crews, however, survived to bask in their glory.

Of all of Hitler's elite units, the German submarine service, or Ubootwaffe, suffered the highest level of casualties. Some 39,000 German submariners put to sea during World War II, and more than 27,000 were killed in action. A further 5000 ended up in Allied prisoner-of-war camps. In total, 754 Unterseeboote or U-boats out of 863 that sailed on operational patrols were lost. In World War I, by comparison, out of 800 U-boats built 343 were lost on patrol and 199 lost in accidents, taking 5249 men with them to the bottom of the sea.

Amid this carnage the Ubootwaffe was no lamb being led to the slaughter: it hunted in fleets, dubbed "wolf packs", and sent just under 2800 Allied ships – 63 percent of all Allied naval losses in the war – to the bottom. In six years of war, it was the Ubootwaffe that came nearest to turning the tide of the conflict in Germany's favour. Up to early 1943, the Ubootwaffe was sinking Allied ships at a greater rate than new ships could be built to replace the losses.

A Type VIIC U-boat returning to her French base from patrol is given an honour guard by the crew of one of her sister boats, February 1944.

Admiral Karl Dönitz had been a U-boat commander in World War I and took over Hitler's new U-boat branch in 1935. He masterminded the U-boat campaign in the Atlantic and became C-in-C of the German Navy in 1943. Loyal to Hitler until the end, he was named the Führer's successor in April 1945.

In the face of such horrendous losses, the men that went to war in Hitler's U-boats needed to be a special breed. They were nominally all "volunteers", who threw themselves into the Battle of the Atlantic with a zeal that was remarkable.

Regulations said that U-boat crews won the privilege of being sent on shore duty after surviving 12 "war cruises" – none ever made it. In return for their efforts a grateful Führer showered the Ubootwaffe with medals, honours, promotions and stardom. It was routine for all crew members to be decorated with the Iron Cross on their return from a war cruise.

U-boat commanders were rewarded even more generously. Even though the officers of the Ubootwaffe made up only five percent of the commissioned officers in the German Navy, they received 50 percent of the Knight's Crosses – Germany's highest decoration – awarded to the Kriegsmarine.

U-boat commanders were intensely competitive, and there was fierce rivalry to sink more ships than their counterparts. The nature of submarine warfare made the U-boat commander a unique type of warrior. In the final stages of a torpedo attack he alone could see the target through his submarine's periscope. The success or failure of the attack was down to the skill and experience of the U-boat commander alone. The Nazi propaganda machine fed the hero worship of these "knights of the deep" or "grey wolves", who went to war in "steel sharks". The rivalry between the U-boat commanders was fed by the award of medals depending on tonnage of ships sunk: 100,000 tonnes (98,400 tons) of shipping sunk got a commander a Knight's Cross, a further 50,000 tonnes (49,200 tons) was rewarded with the Knight's Cross with Oak Leaves. A number of U-boat aces received the Knight's Cross with Swords, and two were rewarded the highly prestigious Knight's Cross with Diamonds.

Dr Josef Goebbels' propaganda was keen to capitalize on the success of the Ubootwaffe, because it was a method of warfare that was distinctly German. The Kaiser's navy had pioneered "unrestricted submarine warfare" against merchant shipping during World War I, and the rise of the Ubootwaffe was proof of the superiority of German military technology and prowess. The Allies had specifically banned Germany from possessing U-boats in the 1919 Treaty of Versailles, so Hitler regarded it as matter of national honour that the Third Reich should rebuild the Ubootwaffe. In 1934 he ordered U-boats to be secretly built and, in 1935, the existence of six was publicly acknowledged. Hitler was seen to be vanquishing the humiliation of Versailles.

KARL DÖNITZ – U-BOAT WIZARD

The man who transformed the Ubootwaffe into the awesome fighting machine it became during World War II was Karl Dönitz who was appointed its head in 1936 at the age of 45. Known as the Befehlshaber de U-Boote (BdU), (commander-in-chief of U-Boats), or "The Lion", Dönitz was a fanatical proponent of the submarine. He commanded U-68 during World War I before being sunk by the Royal Navy off Sicily in October 1918. After going temporarily "insane" in a Scottish prisoner-of-war camp, he was repatriated to Germany. The experience left him with a burning hatred of the British and a desire to prove that, given enough U-boats, their island nation could be brought to its knees.

A U-boat commander begins an attack run, October 1943. By this period of the war there were some 400 U-boats in service, a remarkable achievement considering Dönitz had begun the war with barely 60 boats operational.

In World War I U-boats hunted singly and were defeated when the British instituted their convoy system, which meant escort ships could concentrate their efforts against any single attacker. Dönitz came up with the idea of the Rudeltaktik, or "wolf pack" tactics. This was the centralized control of U-boat attacks by radio. With a force of 300 U-boats, he aimed to isolate Britain by stringing his forces out across the Atlantic to intercept the convoys of merchant vessels. Once a convoy was sighted by a U-boat or a reconnaissance aircraft, a "wolf pack" would converge on the target. Simultaneous attacks from multiple directions would overwhelm the defences.

Before Dönitz could wage his war he needed the right weapons. The 1930-vintage U-boats were small coastal vessels that were incapable of ranging far into the North Atlantic. They were more a symbol than a potent weapon of war. Germany's first submarine had been commissioned in 1906, and during the next 12 years companies such as Krupp Germaniawerft and Blohm & Voss developed considerable expertise producing submarines for the Kaiser. Under Dönitz's direction a programme was implemented that eventually led to the building of 1099 submarines.

Dönitz wanted submarines that could patrol far into the North Atlantic for several weeks at a time. The burden of the U-boat war fell on the Type VIIC boat. This was 66m (221ft) long, had a draft of 4.5m (15ft) and beam of 6m (20 ft 6in). Weighing in at 765 tonnes (769 tons), the Type VIIC could dive in 20 seconds to 100–125m (327–408ft). On the surface it had a speed of 18 knots, but underwater it could only manage 7.7 knots. To operate underwater, the U-boat had to power its engines from electric batteries, which had a very short life. A Type VIIC's batteries had enough power to allow a cruise of only 288km (180 miles) underwater at a speed of two knots.

The 44-man crew of a Type VIIC lived in horrendous conditions throughout their cruise. Food was packed in every spare space of the vessel. Fresh water was strictly rationed and there was none to spare for the purposes of personal hygiene. Far more important than food was making room for the U-boat's 14 torpedoes. Four torpedoes could be fired from forward tubes and there was also a rear-facing aft tube; 88mm and 37mm deck cannons were carried to allow unescorted merchant ships to be sunk without wasting valuable torpedoes.

A Type VIIC boat on patrol in Arctic waters north of Norway. The U-boats were deployed to Norway to help stop the Allied Arctic convoys reaching the Russian port of Murmansk.

Although the Type VIIC was the most numerous type of U-boat, with more than 700 being built, a larger version, the Type IXC, was considered the best long-range German submarine of the war. It weighed in at some 1102 tonnes (1120 tons), had a crew of 54 and could carry 22 torpedoes. This was the submarine that bore the burden of long patrols off the east coast of America and further afield, with more than 150 being built. Some were converted into supply submarines to resupply other U-boats far out at sea. Dubbed "Milk Cows" by the Allies, they were very vulnerable to attack while transferring supplies and nearly all were sunk.

The Achilles' heel of the U-boat was its need to recharge its batteries, which could only be done on the surface to allow carbon monoxide exhaust fumes from the vessel's diesel engines to vent into the atmosphere. Once on the surface, U-boats were vulnerable to detection by radar on Allied escort ships or maritime patrol aircraft. When German troops

overran Dutch shipyards in 1940 they seized experimental examples of a device known as a snorkel. This was a vent that raised like a periscope and allowed the submarine's engines to "breath" while submerged. These began to be fitted on German submarines from 1944.

Just as important as Dönitz's new submarines was the amount of time and effort he put into selecting and training his U-boat captains. These were mainly young naval officers in their late 20s or early 30s, who were selected early in their careers to attend Dönitz's famous Kiel submarine school. Here they learned their trade and earned the right to wear the distinctive white U-boat captain's cap cover. Known as *Herr Kaleu*, from the German rank captain-lieutenant, they were looked on in awe by their crews. Most importantly, crews wished for a lucky *Herr Kaleu* who would bring them glory by sinking enemy ships and then get them home safely.

In the final equation, gaining a "kill" was down to the skill and expertise of the *Herr Kaleu*. This depended on how well a U-boat captain understood the capabilities of his primary weapon system – the torpedo. Known to the Germans as "Eels", the 5m- (5.5yd-) long weapons had a range of some 750m to 1500m (820yd to 1640yd). Their 360kg (800lb) warhead was enough to break the back of a large transport ship, if they could hit the target. German torpedoes had a mechanical guidance system so there was no need to actually point the U-boat at the target, though the captain needed to give the weapon basic bearing and distance information.

Throughout the war the Germans always had problems with their torpedo detonators. They tried both contact and magnetic detonators

An Allied merchant vessel explodes during a convoy run through the Barents Sea. Aerial bombing was the preferred method of German attack on the Allies' Arctic route to Russia. The U-boats, it was decided, were better employed sailing from France against the Atlantic convoys.

with mixed results. As a result, it was a recommended tactic to fire a spread of three to four torpedoes at a target. Data reported that 40 percent of Allied ships went down as a result of one hit, 38 percent to two or more hits, but 22 percent continued sailing after being hit by up to four torpedoes. One improvement was the adoption of battery driven torpedoes to replace compressed air-driven models, which eliminated the tell-tale air bubbles that often alerted Allied sailors to their impending fate, allowing them to take counter-measures. Late in the war the Germans experimented with acoustic torpedoes that homed in on the sound of ships' engines. They proved effective. However, the destruction of two U-boats has been attributed to hits by their own acoustic weapons.

When Hitler invaded Poland in September 1939, Dönitz was far from ready to wage his all-out submarine war against Great Britain. He only had 56 U-boats. Many were useless coastal designs, and only 46 could be considered operational. The U-boat fleet's biggest coup of the so-called "phoney war" period was the sinking of the British battleship *Royal Oak* in the Royal Navy's Scapa Flow anchorage by *U-47*, captained by the famous Gunther Prien, in October 1939. He dodged past the extensive defences undetected to fire on the pride of the Royal Navy's Home Fleet. Prien's first salvo of four torpedoes failed to sink the battleship, so he calmly moved away, reloaded his torpedo tubes and then returned to fire another salvo. This time two found their mark, before Prien was able to make his escape. Hitler was euphoric when he heard the news, and invited Prien and his crew to Berlin to receive medals. *U-47*'s commander became the first *Herr Kaleu* to receive the Knight's Cross.

THE "HAPPY TIME"

Apart from minor actions supporting the German invasion of Norway and Denmark in April 1940, the Ubootwaffe did not contribute to the Blitzkrieg in western Europe. Dönitz, however was very happy to be left in possession of ports on France's Atlantic coast. His U-boats now had direct access to their Atlantic hunting ground. Dönitz began a crash programme to establish his fleet in a series of purpose-built bases at French ports that would be protected from Allied bombers by concrete buildings, called U-boat pens. He set up his BdU command post at Kerneval Chateau, outside the port of Lorient in Brittany, and began directing his U-boats against British shipping convoys.

With German armies poised along the Channel Coast and the Luftwaffe locked in combat with the RAF in the Battle of Britain, the Royal Navy was preoccupied defending the home islands. There were few resources to spare to protect the Atlantic convoy routes, so Dönitz's U-boats were able to move his campaign into a high gear. To the Ubootwaffe, the period from June to October 1940 was "the happy time". They sank 275 ships, weighing some 1.255 million tonnes (1.395 million tons). This exceeded the rate at which Allied shipyards could build replacements and, if it went on for much longer, Great Britain would be starved into submission.

Dönitz's "wolf pack" tactics were proving to be far more effective than he could have imagined. Under the command of an elite cadre of U-boat commanders, such as Otto Kretschmer, Joachim Schepke and Gunther Prien, British convoys were being decimated.

At sea, the U-boats were deployed in "patrol lines" or "interception lines" across the British shipping routes, assisted, if they were within range, by Luftwaffe Focke-Wulf Condor reconnaissance aircraft. When a convoy was sighted, its position would be radioed to Dönitz in his Lorient headquarters. Once the signal had been given, up to 20 U-boats would then be ordered to converge on the position, while the first U-boat would shadow the contact, radioing in a steady stream of reports to ensure that the "wolf pack" did not lose its target.

Attacks were mounted from every direction with both deck guns and torpedoes, usually at night. U-boat captains liked to get as close as

U-67, a Type IXC boat in dry dock in Lorient, France. This type superceded, but did not replace, the VIIC. It was this type which led the successful U-boat offensive against the US east coast in early 1942.

A Type VIIC is loaded with fresh torpedoes inside the massive U-boat pens on France's Atlantic coast. The German censor has crudely removed details of the weapon's propeller and rudder assembly.

possible to their prey, and the most daring ones often submerged and dived under the convoy to attack it from within. With the escorts normally busy on the fringes of the convoy, such attacks took the British completely by surprise and inflicted heavy losses. Some captains even surfaced and daringly engaged targets with their guns to save valuable torpedoes. These tactics also gave the U-boats plenty of time to escape before a response could be organized.

In the autumn of 1940, the toll of Allied ships started to rise alarmingly. And it was not just a case of picking off one or two vessels. Whole convoys suffered horrendous losses, such as Convoy SC7 in October 1940, which lost 30 of 45 ships when it was attacked by eight U-boats. The "wolf pack" barely had time to regroup before another 50-ship convoy entered its area, with the resulting loss of a further 13 ships.

During the next three years Dönitz was able to massively expand his fleet, with 91 U-boats available by the end of 1941. This had doubled to more than 200 in 1942, and when the Battle of the Atlantic reached its climax in the spring of 1943 there were 240 U-boats under Dönitz's command. Some eight flotillas were operating from massive concrete U-boat pens built by the Organisation Todt at Lorient, La Pallice, Brest, Saint Nazaire and Bordeaux.

The war in the Atlantic was not totally one sided, though, with the Royal Navy hitting back hard whenever the Ubootwaffe made a mistake. Prien, the hero of Scapa Flow, died in March 1941 in a depth-charge attack that blew up his submerged U-boat. Ten days later Schepke died when he was forced to surface and a destroyer rammed his submarine; cutting him in half as he stood on the bridge. On the same day Otto Kretschmer was captured. As his U-boat sunk beneath him, Kretschmer calmly smoked a cigar on his bridge as he signalled a Royal Navy ship by lamp to pick up his crew. He was the first U-boat ace to be captured, and was awarded the Knight's Cross with Oak Leaves while in a British prison camp.

As more U-boats took to sea, "the happy time" continued, with 432 Allied ships – 2.03 million tonnes (2 million tons) – being sent to the bottom of the Atlantic in 1941. With the entry of the United States of America into the war in December 1941, the Ubootwaffe were able to prey on unprotected ships along the US eastern seaboard and in the Caribbean. Dönitz dubbed it the "beat of kettle drums" offensive.

In June 1942 U-boats ripped into the Arctic convoy PQ17, and only 11 out of 36 ships made it to their destination in Russia. A total of some 300 ships were sunk in the first six months of 1942, raising the total tonnage sunk in the year to more than 6 million tonnes (5.8 million tons).

This success led to Hitler rewarding Dönitz with command of the German Navy in January 1943, after the sacking of Grand Admiral Erich Raeder. Dönitz's faithful lieutenant, Rear-Admiral Eberhardt Godt, took over the day-to-day direction of the Ubootwaffe, although Dönitz's elevation to the top job meant that the submarine offensive was now the primary focus of the Kriegsmarine's war effort.

In the face of the unrelenting U-boat attacks, the British and US navies were busy developing equipment and tactics to win the Battle of the Atlantic. As well as new escort vessels, sonar-type systems to detect submerged U-boats and mass-produced Liberty

The fruits of victory. Freshly washed and shaved and wearing new uniforms (even if they are British battledress), Captain Otto Kretschmer and the crew of the U-99 receive awards from Admiral Raeder at the Lorient U-boat base.

cargo ships, the British targeted the two main vulnerabilities of Dönitz's "wolf packs" – their radio codes and the U-boats' need to surface to recharge their batteries.

By breaking the German Enigma code system, the British were able to pinpoint the location of all the U-boats at sea, as well as read the orders that Dönitz sent them. This allowed convoys to be routed away from danger and allow counter-measures to be taken.

The decisive weapons against the U-boats were long-range maritime patrol aircraft, such as the British Sunderland and American Catalina flying boats and converted B-24 Liberator bombers. With these aircraft available from 1943 onwards, the "mid-Atlantic gap" was closed, and when the Allies gained access to bases in the Azores in August 1943, the maritime patrol effort intensified. There was now nowhere safe for the U-boats to surface and run on their engines. The installation of radar on the patrol aircraft added to the problems of the Ubootwaffe. RAF Coastal Command went on to sink almost 200 U-boats, just over a quarter of all lost in the war.

THE TURNING POINT OF THE BATTLE OF THE ATLANTIC

In early 1943 Dönitz had more than 400 U-boats in service, more than satisfying the requirements of his prewar plan to defeat Britain. The turning point came in April of that year when the level of U-boat losses started to rise beyond the rate that Dönitz could build new submarines and train new crews. This latter factor was more important than the building of new U-boats, because when the Allies sank one of Dönitz's submarines the whole crew were either all killed or captured. The crews of lost U-boats never made it home. If the loss rates for April 1943, 12 Allied merchant ships lost for 7 U-boats sunk, were alarming for Dönitz, the figures for May were disastrous. He lost 41 U-boats, including one carrying his own son. More than 60 percent of these were claimed by Allied aircraft. On 24 May the Lion recognized that this level was unsustainable and he ordered a withdrawal of the "wolf packs" to southwest of the Azores. The U-boats were no longer the hunters – they were the hunted.

Denied the means to cruise to their patrol areas on the surface and replenish batteries after attacks, the Ubootwaffe was increasingly prevented from operating far from its home bases. Even the introduction of snorkels did not restore the balance, because they could still be detected by airborne radar.

U-boat crews became resigned to having to crash-dive as soon as their lookouts spotted or heard an Allied aircraft. For a time, Dönitz ordered his U-boat captains to try to fight it out on the surface with their cannons and machine guns, but this was usually a futile exercise. Even though the German gunners might be able to drive off the attacking aircraft, Allied warships would soon be on the scene to start depth-charging the U-boat.

Senior officers on deck as a boat returns to base in France after a successful patrol. Their relaxed attitude and the fact that it is broad daylight suggest that this is early in the war. Aggressive Allied air patrols would make this kind of scene nearly impossible later on.

Once submerged, a U-boat captain would try to dive deep and fast, to get away from his pursuers. The slow underwater speed of U-boats meant Allied anti-submarine warships had plenty of time to lay a pattern of depth charges ahead of possible escape routes. U-boat crews had to endure hours of tortuous attack, as their vessel was shaken by shock waves and hull plates buckled. Men verged on madness as "tin can frenzy" gripped crews. If they managed to survive and return to port, they considered themselves very lucky.

The heavy losses and restricted operating areas plunged the Ubootwaffe into a crisis as its veteran commanders and crews were steadily killed off. At the same time, the younger generation of U-boat men were denied the chance to gain experience and invariably ended up dead because they lacked the skills needed to survive. Dönitz's Ubootwaffe was locked in spiral of decline. Knight's Crosses were now rare, and U-boat crews started to call themselves the "children in iron coffins".

The final foray of the U-boats was in June 1944, when Hitler ordered an all-out effort to destroy the Allied invasion fleet off Normandy. Every available U-boat in French ports was ordered to put to sea to take on the 800 ships and 4000 landing craft putting the Allied invasion army ashore. In desperation, they were even ordered to ram Allied ships. The result was a disaster. Only five ships were sunk for the loss of 22 U-boats.

As Allied armies fanned out into France during the summer of 1944, they soon swept into the U-boat ports that had resisted so many air raids. Denied their Atlantic bases, the Ubootwaffe was forced to fall back to bases in Norway and Germany, making it almost impossible for them to reach the Allied convoy routes in the Atlantic Ocean.

In the remaining months of the war, the Ubootwaffe did contribute to efforts to protect evacuation fleets in the Baltic that were lifting German troops and civilians from the advancing Red Army but, for all intents and purposes, their battle in the Atlantic was over.

In a bizarre twist of fate, Hitler, before his suicide in the Berlin bunker in April 1945, named Dönitz as his successor as Führer. The Lion quickly moved to put an end to the war and entered into negotiations to surrender all of Germany's armed forces. On 7 May, Germany's surrender was accepted by the Allies and Dönitz ordered the Ubootwaffe to turn over their 350 vessels to the enemy. Only 156 actually surrendered. The remainder scuttled their U-boats, despite orders from Dönitz. Two U-boat captains even managed make their way to Argentina to avoid Allied captivity. *U-2336*, however, did not receive the surrender order and sank two British ships off the Scottish coast. These were the last U-boat kills of the war.

The Short Sunderland flying boat combined great range and endurance with enough weaponry to sink a U-boat in a single attack. From 1943, constant patrols of both the Sunderland and the B-24 Liberator ensured that Allied Atlantic convoys had air cover from coast to coast.

CHAPTER 5

The "Eighty-Eight" – Top Tank Killer

German 88mm flak gunners were determined and dangerous opponents. Time after time, the 88mm proved the glue that held German defensive positions together. The presence of this awesome weapon, and the determined men who operated it, was a major morale booster to German troops waiting for hordes of Soviet or Allied tanks to attack. Once the 88mms started to rip into the approaching tanks, the enemy attack often ground to a bloody halt.

The armoured shield of this 88 displays its "kill" tally – proving that for a weapon originally designed as an anti-aircraft gun, it could be turned with lethal effect on both enemy armour and fortified bunkers.

In the shimmering morning heat on 15 June 1941, the slow-moving British Matilda "infantry" tanks were waved forward towards the Halfaya Pass, which guarded the Libyan border from British attack. Soldiers of the 11th Indian Brigade were walking behind the Matildas, confident the heavily armoured tanks would provide protection from anything the Germans could throw at them. The British Operation Battleaxe appeared to be going to plan.

Waiting for the 11th Indian Brigade and Matildas were 13 88mm flak guns dug into undulating desert terrain and camouflaged with netting. When the first Matildas hit a hidden minefield and started to have their tracks blown off, the time was ripe for the German gunners to open fire. One squadron of the 5th Royal Tank Regiment was destroyed in the first salvo and the rest of the regiment was soon in retreat. Further attacks by the British 4th Armoured Brigade fared little better. The Matilda's 2-pounder cannons did not have the range to reach the German guns, which were easily picking targets off at more than

1500m (1640yd) range. Even if they could have closed on the German position, the British tanks lacked high-explosive shells because their primary task was to deal with enemy anti-tank gunners by using their machine guns.

In the space of four days the British lost 123 out of 238 of their tanks and failed to budge the Germans from Halfaya Pass. The battle forever destroyed the Matilda's reputation for invulnerability, and soon Allied tank crews came to fear the weapon they called the "Eighty Eight". To their German crews, they were nicknamed the "Acht-Acht" and their presence on the battlefield was a great morale booster. Not only did they keep Allied aircraft at bay, but it was very reassuring for German soldiers to know that they were protected by a weapon that could also defeat any Allied tank. For a gun that was supposed to be an anti-aircraft weapon, the fact that the "Eighty Eight" should achieve fame as an anti-tank gun was no surprise to its designers.

Under the terms of the 1919 Versailles Treaty that ended World War I, Germany was denied the right to possess anti-aircraft artillery. The army of the new Weimar Republic, the Reichswehr, was not going to let such legal niceties get in the way of its plans to develop new weapons. It started to fund the famous armaments firm, Krupp, to set up a secret research base in Sweden in cooperation with the Bofors company. In return, Bofors was invited to set up a branch office in Berlin that was manned solely by Germans. Throughout the 1920s the German designers worked away, preparing for the day when they could openly return to business as usual. Krupp and Rheinmetall were asked towards the end of the decade to design a new anti-aircraft gun, but it was not until 1931 that a satisfactory product was ready. This experimental 88mm gun featured many of the characteristics of the weapon that would be

The 88mm Flak 37 in its original role as an anti-aircraft gun, somewhere on the coast of northern Europe, September 1943. Note the number of ammunition handlers required to keep up the rate of fire (only one crewman actually loaded the gun).

famous in World War II: it had a cruciform wheeled carriage and an 85-degree elevation to fire at aircraft. To fire, the cruciform carriage was lowered to the ground and two elevating side legs dropped to form a firm base. The gun also had a 360-degree rapid traverse.

After the rise of Hitler in 1933, Germany reneged on the Versailles armaments restrictions and Krupp was ordered to begin production of its weapon, designated the 88mm Flak 18. Rheinmetall was then asked by the German Army Weapons Office to come up with a solution to the barrel wear caused by high rates of fire. After 900 rounds, the barrel of the weapon had to be replaced, which meant it had be taken out of use and sent back to depot workshops. The answer was a three-piece barrel that could be replaced in the field. This went into production in 1937 as the 88mm Flak 36. Two years later, a new version, the 88mm Flak 37, with an improved electrical fire control system was introduced, becoming the classic version of the "Eighty Eight".

THE FLAK 18

The basic 88mm Flak 18 weapon weighed 7.1 tonnes (7 tons), which meant it was not easily manhandled once the crew had lowered it from its wheels. Just as famous as the weapon itself was its Kraus-Maffei SdKfz 7 halftrack prime mover, which could carry the gun's crew and a basic load of ammunition.

Operating the weapon was a very labour-intensive process. A single gun was served by a crew of nine, which included a commander, layer to elevate the gun, layer to traverse the gun, a loader, four ammunition handlers, two fuse setters and a tractor driver.

Some of the first guns were sent to Spain with the German Condor Legion to protect the airfields used by General Franco's fascist forces. When they ended up being used against ground targets, the Luftwaffe High Command realized that it needed to order armour-piercing rounds for the weapon and armoured shields to protect their crews from shell fire. These improvements were in hand when war broke out in 1939.

The weapon's high velocity – 820m (2690ft) per second – was the key to its success in both the anti-aircraft and anti-tank roles when supplied with the correct ammunition. For anti-aircraft work, it was provided with time- and pressure-fused high-explosive shells to allow the crew to set the altitude at which the shells exploded. In the ground role, three main types of round were available. The Pzgr 39 armoured-piercing, capped, ballistic cap (APCBC) round was the first round used and was later supplemented by the Gr 38HI high-explosive anti-tank (HEAT) round, and Pzgr 40 armoured-piercing, composite rigid round, which had a tungsten core. With this ammunition an "Acht-Acht" could punch through 99mm (3.8in) of armour at 2011m (2200yd), which meant no type of Allied tank was safe until the arrival of the Soviet Josef Stalin tank in early 1944. Poorly armoured tanks, such as the Sherman and T-34, which had only 51mm (2in) and 47mm (1.8in)

As an anti-aircraft gun the 88 fired pressure-fused and timed high-explosive shells, which depended for their accuracy on the information on the altitude, speed and direction of the enemy aircraft supplied by the battery spotters.

frontal armour respectively, were easy prey for the 88mm at ranges in excess of 3000m (3282yd).

There were a number of attempts to improve on the 88mm Flak 37, including a version with a longer, five-part barrel. A few hundred were built, but technical problems and production delays meant they never replaced the older models in widespread use. The success of the 88mm in the anti-tank role in North Africa and Russia, and the appearance of heavily armoured Soviet T-34s and KV-1s, made the Weapons Office look to producing a specialist anti-tank version. This was a pressing requirement because the existing 50mm and 75mm anti-tank guns were unable to deal with the new Soviet tanks. An important requirement was to reduce the silhouette of the weapon to make it easier for their crews to camouflage and conceal them. The result was the PaK-43, which retained the cruciform carriage of the old 88mm, though this was soon superseded by the PaK-43/41 which was mounted on a single axis carriage, like a traditional artillery piece. While crews liked the killing power of the new anti-tank gun, they were less impressed by its size and weight – more than 6 tonnes (5.9 tons) – and soon nicknamed it the "barn door".

Although a large number of "Flieger-Abwehr-Kanone" or flak units had been formed in World War I, Germany was banned from possessing air defence artillery by the Versailles Treaty. In secret the Reichswehr reformed its flak units in 1928, and disguised them as transport detachments and elements of the German Air Sports Union. Hitler's rise to power in 1933 was quickly followed by the establishment of the German Air Ministry, which was a cover for the secret formation of the

One of the first types of Allied tank to reveal its weakness to the power of the 88 was the British Matilda in northern France in 1940. Still in use in the Western Desert two years later, it proved the desperate need the Allies had for an up-armoured tank.

Luftwaffe. Responsibility for flak units was soon passed from the army to the Luftwaffe, because of the need to integrate anti-aircraft artillery with fighter defences. In only four years the flak branch was expanded to some 115 units, which had the job of defending airfields, key strategic locations and the field army. Two years into the war this number had expanded to 841 units. The flak artillery were divided into static units committed to the defence of the Reich and self-propelled units that accompanied the army into battle. The battalions of self-propelled flak artillery were the elite of the branch and were in the thick of the action throughout the war.

The Army High Command had never been happy with the Luftwaffe having total control of the flak branch, and in 1941 both the Army and Waffen-SS were allowed to form their own flak battalions to be assigned to infantry, panzer, motorized and panzergrenadier divisions. These units had a mixture of 88mm and 20mm or 37mm light flak weapons to protect their divisions from enemy aircraft. However, all matters relating to flak weapons, ammunition and equipment, as well as tactics, doctrine, training and organization, still remained the responsibility of the Luftwaffe flak branch.

While fighter pilots and paratroopers received public adulation as the Luftwaffe's war heroes, the flak gunners were elite non-flying units of the German air force. Operating weapons, such as the "Acht-Acht", in the anti-aircraft role, was very demanding because crews had to be able to understand the complex fire solutions needed to set fuses to explode at high altitude. They also had to work as part of a complex air defence organization so friendly aircraft were not mistakenly engaged. The firing

An 88 and tractor on the open plains of the Western Desert, 1943. The 88 had been designed to be used from fixed, fortified positions, and was never meant to be a mobile element on the battlefield. Its new role as an anti-tank gun exposed the crew to direct enemy fire and necessitated the introduction of a gun shield.

crews had to be fit and determined, firstly, to manhandle their guns into position, dig firing pits and maintain the supply of shells to the gun. Each shell weighed in at more 9kg (20lb) so this was no mean feat.

Gun and battery commanders were highly trained to get the most out of their weapons in the anti-tank role. Once committed to battle the "Acht-Acht" were virtually immobile, so the difference between success or failure depended on the siting of the guns and their concealment until the time came to engage the enemy. Once battle was joined with enemy tanks, flak commanders required strong nerves and faith in the capabilities of the guns and their crews. Outside the cockpit of a fighter or combat as a paratrooper, being a flak gun commander was the quickest way in the Luftwaffe to die for the Führer.

In the first two years of the war, Luftwaffe fighters ruled the skies over Europe's battlefields, relegating flak gunners to relatively straightforward point defence tasks. The brunt of these tasks fell to divisional or corps flak battalions or regiments, which travelled close behind the panzer spearheads. During the Blitzkrieg in France, the Balkans and Russia, divisional "Acht-Acht" batteries were often called upon to engage pockets of enemy tanks that could not be dealt with by the panzer regiment. These were small-scale engagements, involving one or two flak guns being called upon to knock out handfuls of British, French or Soviet heavy tanks that had broken through the German front.

MASSED FLAK BATTERIES

As the Allies and Soviets started to boost their airpower and challenge the Luftwaffe, the Germans began to take air defence more seriously and major resources were put into building up flak batteries. Soviet offensives in the winter of 1942–43 also saw the massed employment of hundreds of T-34s along narrow fronts. In response, the Germans saw the need to field anti-tank defences capable of countering this threat. Massed flak guns were one answer to the growing tank and air threat. Rommel showed what was possible with his use of massed 88mm batteries in the North African desert, and the Germans looked to repeat this success in Russia.

By the summer of 1942, the bulk of 88mm guns in frontline areas had been concentrated in 10 Luftwaffe motorized flak divisions, which were raised to provide air defence for army groups. The divisional flak commander was responsible for the organization of all air defence activity – flak guns, radars, searchlights and fighters – in the army group area. A flak division possessed awesome firepower, usually between 12 to 30 heavy flak batteries, each of four 88mm guns, and a similar number of medium and light batteries, each with a dozen quad 20mm or 37mm cannons.

He, in turn, posted his motorized flak regiments and battalions to key sectors of the front to support a particular army or corps. In times of crisis, they could be concentrated to provide either blanket protection against enemy air forces or a powerful anti-tank emergency

reserve against an armoured breakthrough. If necessary, they could also supplement army artillery battalions in general fire support tasks. Unlike the majority of army artillery units, which were still horse-drawn, the Luftwaffe generously ensured all its flak battalions were fully motorized. With a typical motorized flak regiment mustering more than 20 "Eighty Eights", in effect they were a highly mobile tank-killing force, available to rapidly concentrate firepower at a crucial point on the battlefield if the going got really desperate.

Flak regiments were not committed to the emergency anti-tank role without prior planning and reconnaissance. As a standard procedure, flak commanders would survey their sector of the front for possible firing positions in case enemy tanks broke through. Guns were to be sited to make maximum use of their long range, so clear fields of fire were a must. Overlapping fields of fire were also allocated to individual guns and batteries, so the whole of the front could be swept by fire, creating killing zones. The high silhouette of the 88mm flak gun meant weapons had either to be dug into pits, or hidden in woods and buildings to prevent them being spotted. Good concealment was essential to stop the attackers spotting the flak guns until they were well inside the kill zone and unable to escape. If the enemy spotted the flak guns too soon, then their artillery would fire on the flak batteries with deadly effect.

Essential to the mobility of the 88 and its crew was the SdKfz 7 prime mover. It was one of the heaviest halftracks to see service with the German Army.

The pre-positioning of anti-tank ammunition near to the gun line was very important to ensure that a rapid rate of fire could be maintained for as long as necessary. Flak commanders also liked to have friendly infantry close at hand to protect their guns from enemy ground troops, who might try to infiltrate and destroy them.

Flak commanders identified key points to be defended and concentrated their guns there, to ensure that the defence line held whatever happened. They had to juggle their mission to provide air defence, with the need to counter breakthroughs of enemy armour. Often the requirements of both missions overlapped: for example, defending strategic bridges, railway lines or high ground. Movement to other key sectors on the battlefield was regularly rehearsed so flak units could rapidly move on receiving an accepted codeword.

In emergency situations, a flak commander was usually the first officer on the scene with battle-winning equipment, so they assumed command of the action against the rampaging enemy tanks. Any infantry or troops on the scene subordinated themselves to the flak commander as part of ad hoc battlegroups. No matter how much forward planning had occurred, this was when the flak commander got to show his mettle. They often had to bring order to a chaotic situation, ensuring their guns were in position and fire discipline was maintained until the vital moment. This was a time for iron nerves.

THE BATTLE OF THE MEUSE

The first decisive intervention by "Acht-Acht" guns occurred in May 1940. Heinz Guderian's panzer corps raced to the River Meuse at Sedan to build the bridgehead needed to open a breach in French lines, allowing the panzers to race to the English Channel. Guderian, the father of the German panzers, had the Luftwaffe's Flak Regiment 102 attached for this operation, and gave it a key mission. Colonel von Hippel's regiment had been specially reinforced and trained for its part in an operation that was to turn the battle for France in Germany's favour.

Once the panzers had reached the river, infantry were ordered across in rubber assault boats to seize a bridgehead. French troops and guns emplaced in concrete bunkers high on the far bank were turning the German assembly areas into killing zones. Guderian had already thought about dealing with the French defences, and he had sent his flak gunners to Poland to practice putting shells directly through the firing ports of abandoned Polish bunkers. Covered by panzers, the 88mm crews rolled their guns up to firing positions on the river bank opposite the bridgehead, and started to pick off the French bunkers. In some places the flak gunners were less than 100m (109yd) from their targets, and the 88mm proved to be superbly accurate.

This impressive display of firepower was just the morale boost the assault troops needed as they dropped their boats in the Meuse on 13 May. By the end of the afternoon Guderian had his bridgehead, and during the night the engineers had built the first of several pontoon bridges. The flak gunners moved two 88mms across the river just behind the first panzers and they were soon in action, knocking out French tanks sent to counterattack during the night.

When morning broke, the French and British realized the danger posed by the German bridgehead. Within hours, hundreds of bombers were on their way to put it out of action. Colonel von Hippel's gunners were the only defence available to protect the key bridges. Luftwaffe fighters took on the covering RAF Spitfires, but the bombers pressed home their attacks on the bridges with fanatical bravery. The flak gunners elevated their 88mms and started to pick them off. Wave after wave of bombers were met by a wall of exploding shells. The aircraft that were not hit were forced to abort their bomb runs. By the end of the day, Guderian's bridges were still intact and 112 Allied bombers had been shot from the sky. The panzer general commented that, "our anti-aircraft gunners proved themselves on this day, and shot superbly." A grateful Führer awarded von Hippel with the Knight's Cross.

Erwin Rommel already had experience of using his 88mm flak batteries as an emergency anti-tank force during the Battle of Arras in June 1940, knocking out eight Matildas. At Sidi Rezegh in November 1941, Rommel's flak front stopped the British 7th Armoured Brigade in its tracks, after its commander had rashly ordered his tanks to charge

The PaK-43 was a version of the Flak 37 88mm gun – purposefully designed as an anti-tank weapon. Developed to counter the up-armoured Soviet tanks of 1943–44, it was easier to conceal than its famous predecessor, but its great weight and size made it difficult to manoeuvre.

Passed by an assault gun, either a StuG III or a Jagdpanzer IV, this 88 is positioned on the flank to cover a stretch of exposed road, France 1944.

headlong across the desert directly at the Germans. Only four 88mm guns were dug-in on the first day of the battle and they devastated the British brigade. For reasons best known to the British brigadier, he repeated the exercise over four successive days and some 300 British tanks were left destroyed by the "Acht-Acht" and a group of 50mm anti-tank guns sent to reinforce the flak battery.

Gun crews had to be ready for action at a moment's notice, against unexpected threats. During the battle for the Gazala Line in June 1942 Rommel used his flak guns aggressively, placing batteries close behind the head of his panzer columns. If British tanks were encountered the panzers were to fall back and leave the "Acht-Acht" to deal with them at long range. On the opening day of the battle, the 21st Panzer Division found itself up against 40 of the new American-supplied Grant tanks for the first time. With their 75mm cannon, the Grants out-ranged the German Panzer IIIs and so the latter began a hasty withdrawal away from the new threat. Rommel was close at hand to direct Colonel Wolz's 135th Flak Regiment to steady the German line. Four 88mm guns were quickly formed into an improvised gun line to protect the Afrika Korps' supply trucks. As the Grants got to within 1500m (1640yd), the 88s roared into life. The British tanks started "brewing up", forcing the rest to pull back. Rommel's aggressive use of the 88mm in North Africa established its reputation as a "bogey weapon" in the eyes of British tank crews.

On the Russian Front, German flak units increasingly took on more anti-tank duties as the weight of Soviet offensives increased. The summer of 1943 saw a rejuvenated Soviet armoured force take the offensive after the German Kursk Offensive had been checked. Pre-positioned Soviet tank reserves were unleashed just as the German panzer spearheads had been worn down by anti-tank defences and minefields. With great skill, the Soviet High Command struck at the weak flanks of the German front and, within days, it had been shattered in several places north of Orel. Four Soviet tanks corps smashed through the German Second Panzer Army's front and raced towards the key rail junction at Khotynets. Luftwaffe tank-busting planes and 88mm guns of the 12th Flak Division were the only things that could stop the hundreds of tanks surging southwards. Unless the rail junction was held, panzer reserves would be unable to reach the crisis zone.

FLAK AGAINST T-34S

Although the German fighter-bombers were able to shoot up an entire Soviet tank brigade, more T-34s continued the offensive. A battalion of 88mm guns, already on the move under the cover of darkness, was able to set up a gun line outside Khotynets. When the Soviets tried to stage a coup de main raid on the town they drove into a firestorm of 88mm shells and fell back. More attacks continued over a three-day period, but more "Acht-Acht" batteries arrived to bolster the German defence. Casualties were heavy among the flak gunners, who had to fight off the Soviets virtually unsupported by artillery or armour.

During this desperate battle the division claimed 229 tanks knocked out and ensured the safe arrival of panzer reinforcements, allowing the breaches in the front to be restored. The success of the 12th Flak Division validated the mass employment of the "Acht-Acht" as emergency anti-tank forces.

The next major test of the 88mm came in the summer 1944 on the Normandy Front. In late July the British massed almost 800 tanks around the city of Caen to punch a hole through I SS Panzer Corps' front. A mix of Army, Waffen-SS and Luftwaffe 88mm flak and anti-tank battalions, with some 78 guns, were concentrated in this key sector. In spite of being on the receiving end of saturation bombing by 1000 Allied heavy bombers, the German defences were ready when the first wave of British tanks kicked off Operation Goodwood early on 18 July. The British 11th Armoured Division was sent forward through a 4.8km (3-mile) wide bridgehead. Backed by Tiger and Panther tanks of the Waffen-SS *Leibstandarte* Panzer Division, the surviving "Acht-Acht" gunners emerged from the ruins and started firing into the huge column of British Shermans. By the end of the day more than 300 British tanks were burning in front of the German lines, many of which fell to 88mm flak and PaK-43/41 guns. A renewed attack the following day only resulted in 100 more British tanks being destroyed.

CHAPTER 6

Grossdeutschland –
Armoured Elite

The *Grossdeutschland* Panzer Division was the German Army's premier armoured formation. Staffed exclusively by volunteers, and attracting the cream of Germany's young officers, it quickly established a reputation for excellence on the battlefield. But such elite status meant it was thrown into desperate battles against the Red Army on the Eastern Front, which gradually exhausted its reserves of tanks, armoured personnel carriers and men.

These panzergrenadiers of the *Grossdeutschland* Division make use of a knocked-out Soviet T-34 as a defensive strongpoint. They are facing the Soviet offensive of June 1944, which will see the division in action in the Baltic States.

After Hitler launched his armies at the Soviet Union in June 1941, he increasingly called on so-called "fire brigade" units to spearhead vital attacks or plug gaps in the line after overwhelming Soviet attacks had shattered the German front after 1943.

While the panzer divisions of the Waffen-SS are most commonly thought of as the "Führer's fire brigade", the German Army also created its own elite armoured force. Originally only a motorized infantry regiment, *Grossdeutschland* grew in the space of six years into a panzergrenadier division and then into a huge armoured corps, nominally containing four divisions and two brigades. The *Grossdeutschland* Panzer Corps was destined never to fight together, and many of its units existed only on paper.

The very name *Grossdeutschland*, or Greater Germany, summed up the ethos of the unit. It was no ordinary line unit but the German Army's premier fighting force, containing its most experienced and professional officers and soldiers. It became a matter of pride that the

German Army could field elite units to rival the panzer divisions of the Waffen-SS. The name betrayed the ideological underpinning of the unit – its sole purpose was to lead and win Hitler's war of aggression, first in western Europe and then Russia. *Grossdeutschland* was Hitler's ambition to create a German state that dominated continental Europe. Those nations or races that had no place in the Führer's plans were to be expelled or exterminated. By naming its elite unit after Hitler's maniac scheme, the German Army High Command clearly demonstrated that it had signed up to their Führer's crazed plans to create a "master race". Except for a few small elements, from 1941 onwards *Grossdeutschland* units fought almost exclusively on the Eastern Front against the Red Army.

THE EARLY YEARS

The origins of the *Grossdeutschland* lie in the German Army's Watch or Guard Troops, which were formed in 1934 to secure the High Command's buildings in Berlin. When the Waffen-SS was formed, the army decided to form a rival elite force and the Guard Troops were expanded into a regiment, soon to be named Motorized Infantry Regiment *Grossdeutschland*. This regiment, four battalions strong, was lavishly equipped with trucks, light artillery, mortars and flak and anti-tank guns.

It saw action for the first time during the campaign in France and then spearheaded the German invasion of Yugoslavia in April 1941. Later that summer, it was in the thick of the action as German troops surged into the Soviet Union, advancing into central Russia and then moving south into the Ukraine as part of the force sent to encircle the huge Soviet army defending Kiev. After a brutal winter, holding the front against the Soviet counteroffensive around Moscow, it lost almost 1000 dead and more than 3000 wounded, but established its reputation as the one of the Wehrmacht's most professional and effective fighting units.

In the spring of 1942, orders were issued to expand the regiment into a motorized infantry division, complete with 14 Panzer III and 42 Panzer IV tanks, 21 StuG III assault guns, as well as dozens of SdKfz 251 armoured halftracks, Marder 76.2mm self-propelled anti-tank guns, 88mm flak guns, and towed 170mm and 150mm heavy artillery. The vast majority of the division's infantry still had to travel in soft-skinned trucks and halftracks, so would dismount just outside enemy machine-gun range before going into action on foot. One company of the panzer battalion was equipped with the new Panzer IVF2, which sported the then new L/43 long cannon that was designed to defeat the heavy armour of the Soviet T-34 tank.

The up-gunned and up-armoured Panzer IVF2s would spearhead the *Grossdeutschland*'s advance during the coming summer offensive, dubbed Operation Blue by the High Command. Its aim was to smash

the Soviet armies in southern Russia to open the way for German troops to seize the strategic oil wells in the Caucasus. *Grossdeutschland* was assigned to the Fourth Panzer Army, which was on the most northerly wing of five German armies.

During the advance to the River Don the *Grossdeutschland* panzer crews had a taste of the easy victories experienced during the Blitzkrieg years. The Soviet frontline troops put up the same lamentable performance as the year before and the Germans were soon motoring eastwards. A Soviet tank corps was ordered to counterattack and drive straight into the *Grossdeutschland*, only to be engaged and devastated by the Panzer IVs and IIIs. In the space of a week, some 200 Soviet tanks were knocked out and the Soviet counteroffensive was smashed, trapping 100,000 Red Army soldiers. But the attack was a desperate holding action and it worked. The bulk of the Soviet troops escaped and the *Grossdeutschland* spent the next six weeks chasing ghosts across the empty steppe. Fortunately for the division, it was diverted north to help Army Group Centre around the Rzhev salient rather than joining the Sixth Army for its doomed advance to Stalingrad. Nevertheless, it was not destined to have an easy time. The Rzhev salient pointed towards Moscow and Stalin had ordered a major offensive to destroy it. This was intended as a sequel

An MG 42 team of panzergrenadiers covers the surrender of Soviet soldiers in the first weeks of Operation Barbarossa, July 1941. The *Grossdeutschland* was committed to the fighting in Russia from the very opening of the front.

Heavily camouflaged against air attack, these *Grossdeutschland* Panzer V Panthers begin their rail journey towards the Eastern Front. The Panther was designed to counter the T-34 and first saw action in Russia in July 1943.

to Operation Saturn that had trapped the Sixth Army. The *Grossdeutschland* panzer troops were formed into a hard-hitting reserve that rushed from one crisis point to another, as the salient held through a miserable winter.

In January 1943 *Grossdeutschland* was ordered to be pulled out of the line and moved south to join a major offensive to relieve the Sixth Army. By the time the division made it to its assembly area near Kharkov it was joined by the remainder of the newly formed Panzer Regiment *Grossdeutschland*, which boasted a full battalion of 42 Panzer IVs and a company of 9 new Tiger I heavy tanks. These 58-tonne (57-ton) monster tanks were armed with the deadly 88mm cannon that could destroy a T-34 at 2000m (2188yd). Almost as important, the new arrivals were led by the regiment's commander, Colonel Count Hyazinth von Strachwitz, who was soon to become famous as the "Panzer Count". He was already a hero from World War I, when he had led a German raiding party into Paris.

The division had only just escaped from encirclement in Kharkov, when the newly reinforced panzer regiment was ordered to lead a major German counterattack to turn back the Soviet winter offensive. Von Strachwitz led his panzers forward with considerable dash during March 1943, pushing forward at a great pace until it was engaged by the Soviet II Tank Corps. In the first clash of a bloody week, 46 T-34s were knocked out by the *Grossdeutschland*'s panzer regiment. The German offensive now started to gain momentum, with village after village falling to von Strachwitz's panzers. The following day they ran into a network of Soviet anti-tank guns, called a "pak front" by the Germans, in prepared positions and backed by a large number of infantry bunkers. The Tigers came into their own, standing off and systematically blasting the anti-tank guns out of their bunkers. Flamethrower tanks then finished off the position.

As the attack rolled forward, on 16 March another 30 T-34s were destroyed by the panzers when they surprised a Soviet tank brigade in its assembly area. More Soviet tanks were thrown into the battle two days later, but von Strachwitz heard the tanks coming and quickly deployed his panzers to surprise the advancing Soviets. The panzers were driven into peasant huts to hide them and von Strachwitz ordered his gunners to hold their fire. Soviet tanks cautiously edged forward until they were actually inside the village. With nerves of steel, the panzer crews held fire for several hours. When the Soviet tanks exposed their side armour to the Germans, von Strachwitz fired his 88mm cannon, which took the turret off a T-34 with ease. This was a signal for the rest of the regiment to open up. In a few seconds, 18 T-34s were in flames. It was then that the Germans moved forward to attack. By the end of the day, 90 Soviet tanks had been destroyed. Soviet attacks continued for more than a week as several infantry divisions and tank brigades were thrown at the *Grossdeutschland* lines. All these efforts were rebuffed with heavy losses among the attackers. At the end of March Colonel-General Heinz Guderian, the Inspector-General of the Panzer Troops, came to view the *Grossdeutschland*'s handiwork. With pride, von Strachwitz was able to show the father of the German panzers a tank graveyard north of Kharkov containing hundreds of smashed Soviet T-34s.

KURSK

As heavy rains turned Russia into a mud bath, both the Germans and Soviets turned their attention to reorganizing and refitting their forces for the coming summer campaign season. The Army High Command was determined that *Grossdeutschland* would have the honour of spearheading Operation Citadel to cut off the Soviet defenders holding the Kursk salient, which jutted more than 80km (50 miles) into the German front. It became fashionable among aristocratic, middle-ranking officers to join the *Grossdeutschland* as a way to gain battle experience, medals and promotion. It was also seen as important to ensure the German Army was not totally eclipsed by the Waffen-SS. The rank and file soldiers were now some of the most battle-hardened on the Eastern Front, while a higher than average proportion of the junior officers were Nazi Party members.

Grossdeutschland Panzer IIIs manoeuvre across the open plain during the attack on the Kursk salient, Operation Citadel, July 1943. The *Grossdeutschland* began its part in the battle on 5 July. The halftrack in support is an SdKfz 250.

Grossdeutschland was allocated two battalions of Panther tanks, the newest and most modern tank in the German arsenal. It was developed in response to the T-34 and featured sloped armour and a long-barrel 75mm cannon that was almost as powerful as the 88mm carried in the Tiger. Hitler considered the Panthers crucial to the success of Operation Citadel, and he repeatedly put back the date of the offensive to ensure that 192 of the new "wonder" tanks were ready to lead the attack.

The other elements of the division were also brought up to strength during this period with extra deliveries of tanks, until its two panzer battalions boasted 80 Panzer IVs and 15 Tigers. Enough armoured half-tracks to fully equip *Grossdeutschland*'s armoured infantry, combat engineer or pioneer and reconnaissance battalions were also delivered to the division, together with self-propelled 150mm Hummel and 105mm Wespe howitzers. *Grossdeutschland* was redesignated a panz-ergrenadier division in the days before the Kursk offensive. With four battalions of tanks, the division was the most powerful armoured for-mation on the Eastern Front in July 1943.

Grossdeutschland's panzergrenadiers opened the division's attack on the Kursk salient on 5 July. The first objective was a key piece of high ground needed to open a path for the panzers to roll forward to attack the Soviets' southern flank. The Tiger company led the attack with the new Panthers poised close behind and almost immediately ran into a firestorm of anti-tank fire. An interlocking network of pak fronts had been built by the Soviets all around the Kursk salient. Several Tigers struck mines and had to slug it out with the Soviet anti-tank gunners. To try to move the offensive forward, the Panther tanks were committed, but many soon started to burst into flames. This was not as a result of Soviet fire or mines – the new tanks were proving to have teething troubles. They were, however, easily able to see off a counterattack by a Soviet tank brigade equipped with American-built General Lee tanks.

This set the pattern for the next six days. Rather than being a Blitzkrieg, Operation Citadel turned into a bloody war of attrition. *Grossdeutschland* panzergrenadiers and panzers struggled forward to breach line after line of Soviet defences. Each day they knocked out dozens of Soviets tanks and guns, and took hundreds of prisoners. The cost was grievous, though, with the *Grossdeutschland* Panzer Regiment only able to put 22 Panzer IVs, 38 Panthers and 6 Tigers into the field on 12 July. That was the day the Soviets committed their tank reserves. Hundreds of T-34s surged forward and penetrated the division's front in several places. Panzer counterattacks restored the situation.

The German attack rolled forward again the following day, only to run into fresh pak fronts containing more than 100 dug-in tanks

A *Grossdeutschland* SdKfz 250/2 during the battle for Kursk. This was a halftrack variant used by communications units to lay telephone cables to the frontlines. In a mobile battle such as Citadel, it was an element vital to the successful deployment of a German panzer division.

A *Grossdeutschland* frontline command conference during the battle for Kursk. The officer wears an army-issue armoured crewman's blouse and an issue camouflage helmet cover.

and anti-tank guns. This was just too tough a nut to crack. *Grossdeutschland*'s attack was now stalled.

During the course of the battle the division claimed to have destroyed more than 263 Soviet tanks, 144 anti-tank guns, 22 artillery pieces and 11 multiple rocket launchers. *Grossdeutschland*'s own tank losses were a modest 10 Panzers IVs and 43 Panthers, but scores of other vehicles were damaged and unfit for action. Less than a third of the tanks that went into action on 5 July were ready for action. Losses among the division's panzergrenadiers were equally grievous.

With Operation Citadel bogged down the Soviets now launched their strategic reserves against the northern German attack force. It was soon reeling back in disorder, so Hitler ordered *Grossdeutschland* to be pulled out of the line to move north to restore the situation. The division had barely time to unload its vehicles and equipment from its railway flat cars when another massive Soviet offensive broke through the German lines around Kharkov, and so it was on its way southwards to help plug the gap in the line.

HOLDING THE LINE

Four Soviet armies had smashed open a breach 80km (50 miles) wide in the Fourth Panzer Army's front and more than 2000 T-34s were motoring southwards. While the Waffen-SS panzer divisions *Totenkopf* and *Das Reich* attacked from the south, *Grossdeutschland* and 7th Panzer were to hit the northern flank of the Soviet advance. As the division gathered for its attack, the newly-formed Tiger battalion joined von Strachwitz's regiment. He had more than 100 tanks, including some 40 Panthers, 40 Tigers and 30 Panzer IVs. The *Grossdeutschland* started to be called a "super panzer division", even though it was officially still a panzergrenadier division, because it boasted the strongest tank force in the German Army.

Once committed to action, the division found itself engaged in a swirling tank battle against waves of hundreds of T-34s advancing across an almost flat steppe. Tigers and Panthers picked off the Soviet tanks at extreme range in cornfields, while the *Grossdeutschland*'s panzergrenadiers had to fight off human-wave attacks of Soviet infantry. Daily kill rates of 40–50 T-34s were recorded during this period, creating major problems for the division's maintenance crews who had to institute a crash programme to repair worn-out tank cannon barrels.

The counterattack at Achtyrka was a major tactical success for *Grossdeutschland*, but the remainder of the German front was still weak and a retreat to the River Dnieper was ordered. *Grossdeutschland* formed the rearguard as Army Group South pulled back. The Soviets gave the Germans no respite, though, and they were soon across this mighty river barrier. For three months *Grossdeutschland* found itself being rushed from one crisis zone to another as the Soviet steamroller ground forward. By March 1944, the German front had been pushed back to the Romanian border and the Soviets at last seemed to run out of steam, giving the Germans a chance to reform and regroup their battered divisions. *Grossdeutschland* was now led by Lieutenant-General Hasso von Manteuffel, perhaps its most famous commander. Although only 1.5m (5ft) tall, the aristocratic officer was a bundle of energy and led his division from the turret of a Panther tank.

By late April, von Manteuffel had been able to concentrate his division around the border town of Targul Frumos and build up a strong defensive position. His panzergrenadiers were deployed forward, holding a network of trenches and bunkers to hold off the Soviet infantry. Artillery batteries were positioned to sweep the division's front with fire, and 88mm flak guns were dug-in to deal with any enemy armour that broke through the frontline. Von Manteuffel held his panzer regiment, with 25 serviceable Panzer IVs, 10 Tigers and 12 Panthers, plus an assault gun battalion, with 25 StuG IIIs, in reserve. He located his command post on a hilltop overlooking the whole of his sector. The scene was set for a one of the classic defensive battles on the Eastern Front.

After spending a day blasting the German lines with rolling salvoes of artillery fire, the first Soviet tank attacks went in on 2 May. The panzergrenadiers on the frontline allowed the first wave of 25 T-34s to pass over their trenches and let the 88mms take them on. More than half fell

A *Grossdeutschland* Pak 38 team and tractor prepare their gun for action. The anti-tank element was an essential part of any panzer division. As the Pak 38 had an effective range of only 2000m (2188yd), this photograph was taken either on or close to the frontline.

to the flak gunners and the remainder were easily finished off by panzers. Another probe by 30 T-34s was destroyed for no loss by the assault gun battalion, which ambushed them from a hull-down position on a ridge just behind the German front.

The Soviets than committed seven of their Josef Stalin II heavy tanks armed with 122mm cannons, which began engaging von Manteuffel's panzer group at more than 3000m (3282yd) range. The Tigers were called up to drive them off, but their 88mm rounds simply bounced off the armour of the new Soviet tanks. They had to advance to under 1800m (1969yd) before they managed to punch through the weaker side armour of four of the Josef Stalin tanks. Pursuing Panzer IVs destroyed them as they turned tail.

Another Soviet thrust managed to break into a village on the right flank of the division and then more T-34s surged into the breach. Von Manteuffel led a Panzer IV company to the critical sector, knocking out 30 Soviet tanks and driving off the rest.

For two more days, this pattern was repeated with massive Soviet tank and infantry attacks along the *Grossdeutschland* front. Time and again, von Manteuffel's frontline troops held their nerve until the panzers rode to the rescue. On 5 May, the Soviets pulled back. They left the remains of 350 destroyed tanks, and von Manteuffel estimated a further 200 Soviet vehicles were damaged. Just 10 German tanks were lost.

LAST STAND

The following month, in June 1944, the biggest Soviet offensive of the war smashed the German Army Group Centre and ripped open a huge gap in the Eastern Front. German troops were driven from Soviet territory and retreated back into Poland. By 1 August 1944 Red Army troops had reached the Baltic, cutting off Army Group North around Riga. The situation was desperate. *Grossdeutschland* was called upon to spearhead an effort to reopen a land route to the trapped troops.

After safely unloading from its trains, the division was first sent to destroy a Soviet Guards Tank Corps at Wilkowishken on the East Prussian border with Lithuania. Some 350 tanks and other *Grossdeutschland* armoured vehicles were launched into action, and soon found that they were up against hundreds of heavily armoured Josef Stalin tanks, backed up by SU 100 and SU 122/152 heavy assault guns. Avoiding a head-to-head fight, von Manteuffel manoeuvred his outnumbered tanks to fire on the weak side armour of the Soviet vehicles. The Soviets eventually withdrew, leaving some 70 tanks and 60 anti-tanks guns behind.

Towards the end of August, the division was ready to spearhead the drive to open a corridor to Riga. Some initial penetrations were made but the Soviet defences were just too strong. When the attack ground to a halt on 23 August, all the division's tanks were out of

The *Grossdeutschland*'s commander from January 1944 was General von Manteuffel (left), who after his successes with the 7th Panzer Division was promoted to lieutenant-general and given command of what was the German Army's elite panzer unit.

A Panther (possibly an Ausf G) and panzergrenadiers of the *Grossdeutschland* wait to advance in the mid-summer heat. Russia, August 1944. By this time the Soviets were on the borders of Poland and the division was involved in a series of desperate "fire-fighting" operations.

action, either destroyed or under repair. Only when new Tigers and Panthers arrived could the panzer regiment be considered fit for offensive action.

The Soviets had by now gathered 19 infantry divisions and 5 tank corps to renew the offensive and when they struck in October, the weak divisions around *Grossdeutschland* collapsed. For several days the division was effectively surrounded. Under protection of its Tigers and Panthers, *Grossdeutschland* managed to form a rearguard to allow several other German divisions to pull back into Memel. *Grossdeutschland* then withdrew, with Soviet tanks hard on its heels. The town was dubbed a "fortress" by Hitler but this was a myth. It was a hell-hole, bombarded relentlessly by Soviet guns. Eventually its garrison, including the remnants of *Grossdeutschland*, were withdrawn by sea to East Prussia.

As it reorganized in East Prussia during December 1944, the division was ordered to detach several units to help form the Panzer Corps *Grossdeutschland*. On paper this was supposed to contain the original *Grossdeutschland* Division, the panzergrenadier divisions *Brandenburg* and *Kurmark*, the Luftwaffe panzer division *Hermann Goering*, along with the *Führer* Grenadier and *Führer Begleit* brigades. These units were never to go into action together. Combat losses and supply shortages meant they never received anything like enough equipment and men to replace the horrendous losses at the front.

When the next Soviet offensive broke in the middle of January 1945, a much-depleted *Grossdeutschland* Division rolled into action for the last time. Heavy fighting raged for weeks in the woods and forests of East Prussia as the division steadily fell back towards Königsberg. On 17 March the last panzer counterattack was launched by three of the division's Tigers to protect its precarious toehold on the Baltic coast. Their crews fought to the last to screen the evacuation of their comrades to the Samland peninsula. For almost a month the division's survivors fought on here as infantry until they were finally evacuated by ship to Denmark. In the space of three months more than 17,000 *Grossdeutschland* soldiers were killed in action. Only a few hundred men of the division made it to the relative safety of British captivity.

It was typical of the *Grossdeutschland* Division that it went down fighting. As the German Army's elite panzer unit it was created to spearhead Hitler's war of conquest in the East. When the Blitzkrieg faltered, time and again the division was thrown into the breach to hold the Eastern Front together. Equipped with the latest and most powerful tanks Germany's factories could build, *Grossdeutschland*'s panzer regiment regularly achieved amazing tactical success. Only in the autumn of 1944, when the Soviets fielded huge numbers of their monster Josef Stalin tanks, did the division's panzer crews find themselves the prey rather than the hunters.

By the winter of 1944–45 the *Grossdeutschland* was fighting on the Baltic coast of East Prussia, and launched its final offensive around Königsberg in March. It was a fight to the finish, and the survivors who managed to escape to Denmark numbered only a few hundred.

Tigers –
The Heavy Punch

The Tiger I heavy tank was the most famous tank of World War II.
Built in relatively few numbers, rather slow and prone to mechanical
problems, its 88mm gun and heavy armour made it a feared oppo-
nent on the battlefield. In the hands of a panzer ace such as Michael
Wittmann it became almost invincible. The Tiger II tank, on the
other hand, was less of a legend, and most fell prey to mechanical
problems rather than Allied anti-tank rounds.

No tank epitomized the German panzer force better than the
Tiger tank. The mere presence of a single Tiger on a World War
II battlefield would send Allied tanks crews into a panic. These
armoured monsters were almost invulnerable to Allied anti-tank
weapons, and their powerful 88mm cannons could cut through the
armour of American Shermans or Soviet T-34s like a hot knife through
butter. On top of their armour and firepower superiority, German
Tigers were always manned by the best panzer commanders and crews
in the Third Reich, who were highly skilled at getting the best out of
their machines.

Thankfully for the Allies, they never had to face large numbers of
Tigers. The monster tanks were expensive and difficult to build, while
Allied bombing further delayed and disrupted production. Germany's
reputation for its superb engineering even worked against the Tiger. Its
very complexity, for example, made it hard to maintain, so that more
were lost to breakdowns than enemy action.

SS-Obersturmführer (Lieutenant)
Michael Wittmann. This Tiger "ace"
already had 117 confirmed tank kills
from the Eastern Front when he
arrived in Normandy in June 1944, as
commander of 2 Kompanie, 101st SS
Heavy Panzer Battalion.

There was more than one member of the Tiger family, which grew to include two tanks and two monster assault guns. This, however, was more by accident than design. The titans of the German armaments industry, Henschel, MAN, Daimler Benz and Porsche, all produced designs for heavy tanks during the late 1930s, as they rushed to win contracts to produce the weapons needed in Hitler's rearmament programme.

Not much happened until late 1941, when the appearance of the T-34 in Russia caused a major panic. The new Soviet tank had revolutionary sloped armour, a powerful 76mm cannon and the Christie suspension system. German weapon procurement was in a highly chaotic state, the German Army's weapons office placing an order with Henschel for its design of a new heavy tank and Hitler later being swayed by Dr Ferdinand Porsche to give the go-ahead for his design.

TIGER PRODUCTION

Eventually the modified Henschel design got permission to proceed, and later became known as the Tiger E or Tiger I after production began in August 1942. Some 1300 were built before construction ceased two years later. Some 90 Porsche chassis had already been built by the time the project was cancelled, and so they were later converted into assault guns armed with fixed 88mm cannons. A version of the Tiger I fitted with a 380mm mortar for demolition work was also built in small numbers. Late in 1942 work began to develop a new improved version, the Tiger II or King Tiger, with heavier sloped armour and a more powerful version of the 88mm cannon. Henschel and Porsche again competed and the former won. Different turret versions, however, were eventually built by both companies. Just under 490 Tiger IIs were built from January 1944 until March 1945. Weighing in at 71 tonnes (70 tons), compared to 58 tonnes (57 tons) for a Tiger I, the Tiger II was the heaviest German tank to actually see combat during the war. The final version of the Tiger family was the Jagdtiger tank hunter, which was based on a Tiger II chassis and sported a fixed 128mm cannon. Only 80 were eventually built.

Everything about the Tiger was impressive. The frontal armour of the Tiger I was 100mm (4in) thick and impenetrable to almost every Allied anti-tank weapon until 1944, when the British 17-pounder and Soviet 122mm guns appeared. In 1943 one Tiger on the Russian Front reported surviving 227 anti-tank rifle hits, 14 52mm shell hits and 11 7.62mm anti-tank guns hits – none of which penetrated the tank's armour. The Tiger II was even better protected, with 180mm (7in) frontal armour that was sloped. This made the monster impossible to knock out except by attacking its side armour. The L/56 88mm carried by the Tiger I, and later the L/71 88mm of the Tiger II, were superb weapons that were able to destroy all but the most heavily armoured Allied or Soviet tanks, such as the Churchill or Josef Stalin, at ranges in excess of 2000m (2188yd).

The Tiger I and II were designed along conventional lines, with the main armament mounted in a rotating turret. They both required a crew of five: a commander, gunner, loader, driver and a hull machine gunner/radio operator. Fighting inside the Tiger was often a confusing and terrifying experience. When closed down for battle, the crew could only view the world through their small vision ports or periscopes. Only constant running commentaries from other tank crews over the radio kept them fully abreast of what was happening around their vehicle. When enemy infantry got close or anti-tank fire started bouncing off the armour, Tiger crews became very nervous. Mutual support from other Tigers often proved the best protection.

The tank's sheer bulk created new challenges for the Tiger crews. The tank's great weight of armour put a heavy strain on the engines, transmissions and tracks. Maintenance was a nightmare, and crews had to spend far more time keeping them going than other German tanks. If one Tiger should break down, the only way to recover one was with another Tiger. As the German Army began its long retreat from Russia in 1943, it was very common for broken-down Tigers to be abandoned because they could not be moved.

Initially it was intended to provide every panzer regiment with its own company of about a dozen Tigers, but soon afterwards the Army High Command decided this was a mistake. The Tigers were to be concentrated in independent heavy tank battalions, containing some 45 vehicles, for decisive shock action. Tigers were intended to be used en masse to overwhelm opponents with firepower. The new battalions were to be assigned to panzer corps for specific operations, rather than

Prototypes of the Panzer VI underwent trials in April 1942 and production began in August. The Henschel company supplied the chassis and operating systems, Krupp the turret and gun assembly. Porsche provided the tank's popular name: "Tiger".

The Tiger was rushed into service on the Eastern Front in August 1942, and lacking experienced crews and suitable tactics fared badly. Committed in large numbers during the Battle of Kursk the following July, the Tiger (above) revealed its true worth.

parceled out to individual panzer divisions. The Waffen-SS *Leibstandarte*, *Das Reich* and *Totenkopf* Divisions, as well as the army's *Grossdeutschland*, had already formed their Tiger companies before the new structure was decided on, so they had small detachments of Tigers for most of 1943 until they could be expanded to battalion strength.

From the beginning it was envisaged that the Tiger battalions would be the elite of the German Army's panzer troops. Only veteran panzer crews were posted to the new units when they began forming in early 1942, while the first Tigers were still on the Henschel production line at Cassel. The first two companies were formed in February 1942, and by May moves were made to activate the first three heavy battalions even before production tanks were ready. As the new tanks began to take shape the Tiger crews were sent to the factory to spend several weeks helping to build them, so they could master every intricacy of their construction. In the factory grounds and proving grounds, the crews put the Tigers through their paces for the first time. They then took their tanks to training grounds around Germany to learn how to drive, maintain and fight their new vehicles. The gunners zeroed their weapons, commanders tested out basic tactics, and drivers got the measure of their new charges.

It was intended only to commit the new units to battle when they were fully trained and equipped, so they could have a decisive impact and achieve maximum surprise over the enemy. Hitler, however, was impatient for his new toys to see action and so, in August 1942, ordered four Tigers of the 502nd Heavy Tank Battalion to move immediately to join the attack on Leningrad. The tank crews were not yet fully trained and, not surprisingly, the deployment was not a success. On their first mission, the tanks got stuck in swampy ground and had to be abandoned by their crews. Eventually three were recovered and the remaining tank was destroyed to prevent it falling into enemy hands. It was a far from impressive performance, and confirmed the Army High Command's view on how the Tigers should be employed en masse.

TIGER TACTICS

By the end of 1942 the Tiger force was ready for battle, and the Soviet winter offensive provided ample opportunity for the new tanks to prove their worth. On the Leningrad Front in January 1943, the 502nd Heavy Tank Battalion's detached company found itself called to rescue an infantry division being overrun by 24 T-34s. When the "Snow Tigers" arrived on the scene they were able to pick off 12 of the Soviet tanks at long range for no loss. For over three months, the Soviets sent in attack after attack against the same stretch of front, providing the Tigers with easy pickings. When a Soviet attack materialized, the "Snow Tigers" would drive forward from their hides to firing positions behind the German infantry and devastate the T-34 attack waves before they could reach the forward edge of the German line. During this time the Tiger company claimed more than 150 kills, beginning the legend of the "Tiger ace".

In southern Russia, Field Marshal Erich von Manstein was soon to launch his famous counteroffensive to drive back the Soviet armies from the eastern Ukraine. The Waffen-SS and *Grossdeutschland* Tiger companies were to be in the thick of this action, when his panzer divisions turned on their pursuers in February 1943 and advanced to retake the city of Kharkov.

Exhausted by nearly three months of continuous offensive action and short on supplies, the Soviet armies in the Ukraine were in no condition to resist von Manstein's panzer strike. In the first days of the offensive, German panzer units took the Soviet columns by surprise, catching anti-tank guns still attached to towing vehicles and tanks stuck between supply trucks. Von Manstein's panzers enjoyed easy prey, shooting up almost defenceless convoys of panicked enemy troops. As the drive north to Kharkov gathered momentum the Tigers were in the lead. Now the Soviets had recovered their composure and the Germans began to run into whole brigades of anti-tank guns, dubbed "pak fronts", dug into prepared positions and backed by scores of T-34s. The Tigers came into their own, because they were the only German tanks that could engage the pak fronts from a safe distance. If a direct frontal assault was required, then the Tigers could

A Tiger of the *Das Reich* Division on the Eastern Front, February 1943. Extra-wide tracks have been fitted to allow the tank's 58 tonnes (57 tons) to manoeuvre in the winter mud.

also safely advance and overrun the Soviet gun line. More lightly armoured tanks, halftracks and self-propelled guns followed in close behind, ready to exploit any gaps created by the Tigers. This tactic became known as the "panzer wedge".

This tactic came into its own during Operation Citadel, the Battle of Kursk, when the Soviets deployed so many interlocking pak fronts that it was impossible to outflank them. The only thing for the Germans to do was to try to batter their way through by pushing the Tigers to the fore. At Kursk the Tigers made easy work of the pak fronts, but it was slow work and losses were heavy. Huge minefields protecting the Soviet positions slowed the advance and knocked out many of the Tigers. Pioneers had to be repeatedly called forward to clear a path through the Soviet minefields, so the advance could begin again.

A week into Operation Citadel the Tiger force was badly depleted, with only a handful of operational tanks left in each company. Only superhuman efforts by

At the end of 1942, Tiger battalions were sent to bolster Afrika Korps operations in Tunisia. It was here that British and American tank crews first learnt that their Sherman and Grant tanks were no match for it.

repair crews, who night after night ventured onto the battlefield to get the damaged tanks working again, kept the Tiger force in action. The tank crews were worn out and exhausted after continuous action. The offensive was fully defeated on 12 July after the Soviets committed their strategic reserves during the Battle of Prokhorovka. In the largest tank engagement of the war, more than 850 Soviet tanks surged forward in huge waves against II SS Panzer Corps. Across a flat open steppe, the brunt of the attack fell on the *Leibstandarte*'s panzer regiment. With barely 70 tanks and assault guns, including only four Tigers, the regiment fought a desperate action throughout the day, taking on and defeating wave after wave of Soviet tanks. The Tigers' 88mm cannons gave the *Leibstandarte* a huge range advantage, allowing Soviet tank brigades to be decimated before they got to within firing range of the German lines. Almost 200 Soviet tanks lay burning in front of the division at the end of the day. One Waffen-SS Tiger commander, Michael Wittmann, established his reputation as one of the war's best tank commanders during the fighting at Kursk. His kill total by the end of the battle was 30 tanks and 28 anti-tank guns.

After Kursk, Hitler's armies were forced on the defensive in Russia and a growing number of Tigers were assigned to the Eastern Front, where they played a vital role in the futile German attempt to hold back the Soviet steamroller. Tiger battalions were thrown into a series of desperate battles, often holding long sections of front against overwhelming odds. However, during the winter of 1943–44, the effect of unending combat, mechanical breakdowns and unreliable supply lines meant Tiger battalions could often only put a dozen tanks into the field.

German commanders kept them back as a reserve to counterattack against Soviet breakthroughs, and only committed the Tigers once the focus of the Red Army attack had been properly identified. Then the Tigers rolled. These engagements quickly became deadly stalks, as pairs of Tigers often found themselves up against hundreds of T-34s. A pair of Tigers would usually be assigned a sector to hold and clear of enemy tanks. One Tiger would move into an over-watch position to cover its partner as it moved forward. When this tank reached cover, it would stand firm and the second tank would move forward to find another fire position. Tiger commanders usually stood up in their turrets, scanning the horizon for targets with binoculars, despite the risk from snipers or artillery fire. Once the enemy was detected, the Tiger

A Tiger I of the SS *Totenkopf* Division operating in Russia, summer of 1944. The hull is covered with an anti-magnetic compound called "Zimmerit" to protect the tank against magnetic mines, a practice that was phased out by 1945.

A Tiger I in rather worn white camouflage paint, Eastern Front, early 1944. Winter uniforms had improved by this stage of the war and the commander wears a reversible camouflage parka. His steel helmet is attached to the turret on his left.

commander would try to find a firing position to engage the enemy from the flank. While the Tiger's 88mm cannon could be counted on to penetrate the front armour of almost all Soviet tanks, there were still sound tactical reasons for flank attacks. Soviet tanks had poor optical systems and few radios, so unless a target was to their front there was little chance it would be spotted. Even if one Soviet tank commander spotted a target, there was no way to share the information with other tanks.

From concealed firing positions, Tigers regularly reaped a deadly harvest of death against Soviet tank columns. Often the Russians had no idea what was happening for several minutes as Tiger fire started to rip into T-34 after T-34. Even if the Tigers were spotted, the Soviets could rarely coordinate an effective response. By then the Tigers were already pulling back into cover and moving to a new fire position, leaving burning Soviet tanks behind them.

The arrival of heavily armoured Josef Stalin tanks in early 1944 made it even more important for the Tigers to use guile to stalk their prey. It was now vital for the Tigers to get the first shot in.

In the West, Tigers retained their armour and firepower supremacy and could hold their own against vast numbers of Allied tanks. Wittmann on one occasion even engaged a whole British armoured brigade by himself and destroyed 25 Cromwell tanks, stopping a division attack in its tracks.

The greatest threat to the Tiger in the West was from Allied air supremacy. Camouflage and concealment was the best defence against prowling squadrons of rocket-armed Typhoons. During the Normandy campaign in 1944, Tigers operated from hides in woods or farm buildings and would only move forward to the front when an attack was imminent. Once they had completed their task, they would quickly move back to cover.

During the December 1944 Ardennes Offensive, the mountainous terrain and limited number of roads meant unusual tactics had to be adopted by the Waffen-SS Tiger II battalion, attached to the *Leibstandarte* Division. The unit spearheaded the advance of Joachim Peiper's battlegroup into the heart of the American defences. With no room to deploy offroad, Peiper put his Tiger IIs at the head of his column. Even though this slowed up the advance it meant that whenever his columns ran into opposition, the Tiger IIs easily blasted a way through. American anti-tank gunners could only watch in horror as their shells literally bounced off the front armour of the German monsters.

What of the individual Tiger battalions? The 501st Heavy Panzer Battalion was formed in the summer of 1942. The battalion took its tanks to North Africa in December 1942 and clashed with British and American troops until it surrendered in May 1943. The unit was reformed and sent to Russia in November 1943, and fought there until

Michael Wittmann (far left) and his Tiger crew in Russia, winter 1943–44. All wear the Iron Cross and Tank Battle awards. The crew's "kills" can be seen recorded on the cannon barrel above them. Wittmann received the Knight's Cross for these victories on 14 January 1944.

Mechanics prepare a track change on a Tiger I. The Tiger could only be transported by rail by fitting narrow 52cm (20in) transit tracks, which fitted the width of a flat car. Wider 72cm (28in) tracks were fitted for frontline operations.

it was decimated in the Soviet offensive that destroyed Army Group Centre in July 1944. After being reformed with Tiger IIs, it was sent to the Eastern Front again as the redesignated 424th Battalion.

502nd Heavy Panzer Battalion

The first Tiger I unit to be formed, it was the first one to see action on the Leningrad Front in August 1942. It remained in action on the northern sector of the Eastern Front until the end of the war. In January 1945 it was redesignated the 511th Heavy Panzer Battalion.

503rd Heavy Panzer Battalion

Perhaps the most effective Tiger unit of the war after it was sent to join Army Group South in January 1943, where it spearheaded von Manstein's winter counteroffensive. It then saw constant action as part of III Panzer Corps during the Battle of Kursk and the retreat to the Dnieper. In January 1944 it was grouped together with a Panther battalion to form Heavy Panzer Regiment *Bake*, under

the command of Lieutenant-Colonel Dr Franz Bake. This regiment neutralized a pocket of 267 Soviet tanks and then spearheaded the German relief attempt to free the Korsun-Cherkassy Pocket. After being decimated later in the spring, the battalion was reformed and sent to fight in Normandy. In the autumn of 1944 the unit was re-equipped with Tigers IIs and sent back to the East as the Feldherrenhalle Heavy Panzer Battalion. It was trapped in Budapest in January 1945 by the Soviet winter offensive and destroyed. A new 503rd Battalion was formed in early 1945 and sent to fight with Army Group Vistula until the end of the war.

504th Heavy Panzer Battalion

Most of this unit was sent to Tunisia in January 1943, where it was destroyed. Some elements survived and fought in Sicily, and it was reinforced to help defend Italy as part of the *Hermann Goering* Panzergrenadier Division. The units remained there until the end of the war.

A Tiger Ausf E of 1 Kompanie, 101st SS Heavy Panzer Battalion, moves through a Normandy village east of Rouen towards the Allied front, June 1944. The 101st had moved from Paris on 8 June and arrived at the front on 13 June.

505th Heavy Panzer Battalion

Dispatched to join Army Group Centre in the late spring of 1943, it then spearheaded the offensive against the northern front of the Kursk salient. It remained in this sector until the following summer, when it was almost destroyed during the Soviet summer offensive. Re-equipped with Tiger IIs, it fought to the end in East Prussia.

506th Heavy Panzer Battalion

Committed to fight with Army Group South in the autumn of 1943, the battalion fought in the Ukraine until the summer of 1944 when it was withdrawn and re-equipped with Tiger IIs, and was sent to help defeat the Allied airborne landings in Holland in September 1944. In December it was assigned to support the I SS Panzer Corps during the battles in the Ardennes and Hungary.

507th Heavy Panzer Battalion

Formed in September 1943, the unit was committed to the Eastern Front the following January and served there until February 1945, when it was re-equipped with Tiger IIs while still in the line.

508th Heavy Panzer Battalion

Sent to Italy in January 1944, the battalion spearheaded the German offensive against the Allied bridgehead in Anzio. It remained in Italy for a year until it was decided to pull it back to Germany to be re-equipped with Tiger IIs. The unit was then sent to fight on the Western Front.

509th Heavy Panzer Battalion

Ordered to the Eastern Front in November 1943, the battalion fought there for almost a year until it was withdrawn to be re-equipped with Tiger IIs, before being sent to fight in Hungary in January 1945.

510th Heavy Panzer Battalion

One of the last Tiger I battalions, it was formed in June 1944 before being rushed to the East to try to halt the Soviet summer offensive in the central sec-

Only one unit of Tiger IIs was available to counter the Normandy invasion: 1 Kompanie, 503rd Heavy Panzer Battalion. In August 1944 it moved from eastern France, but due to Allied air attacks only 12 tanks arrived at the front.

tor. It remained there fighting the Soviets until the end of the war.

301st Heavy Panzer Battalion
Equipped with both the Tiger I and the BIV remote-control demolition robot vehicles, the unit was formed in the summer of 1944. Sent to the West in November 1944 it saw action during the Ardennes Offensive, where it was all but destroyed.

Kummersdorf Panzer Battalion
A scratch unit that was formed to defend Berlin in February 1945, it went into action with the *Munchenberg* Panzer Division the following April and was destroyed as Soviet troops swept into Berlin.

GROSSDEUTSCHLAND
III Battalion/Panzer Regiment
Grossdeutschland
During the first half of 1943, the elite army division had only a single Tiger I company, but it was later

joined by a full Tiger battalion late in the summer. The battalion fought with the division for remainder of the war.

WAFFEN-SS
SS Heavy Panzer Companies
The *Leibstandarte*, *Totenkopf* and *Das Reich* Divisions were all provided with Tiger I companies in late 1942, and saw action on the Eastern Front throughout the following year.

101st SS Heavy Panzer Battalion
(later redesignated 501st)
Formed from the *Leibstandarte*'s Tiger company in the autumn of 1943 as the heavy battalion assigned to the newly formed I SS Panzer Corps. It was ready for action when the corps was sent to defend Normandy in June 1944. Michael Wittmann eventually commanded the unit until he was killed in action near Caen. It was later re-equipped with Tiger IIs and saw action in the Ardennes and Hungary.

At 71 tonnes (70 tons), the Tiger II (the King or Royal Tiger) was the heaviest tank to see combat operations in World War II. It entered service on the Eastern Front in May 1944 armed with a long 88mm L/71 gun and three machine guns.

102nd SS Heavy Panzer Battalion (later redesignated 502nd)

Formed to support II SS Panzer Corps, the unit saw action in Normandy from July 1944 onwards. By the end of 1944 it had been re-equipped with Tiger IIs.

103rd SS Heavy Panzer Battalion (later redesignated 503rd)

Originally formed with Tiger Is in 1943, it never saw action and was eventually re-equipped with Tiger IIs. It was then ordered to the Eastern Front.

653rd and 654th Panzerjäger Battalions

Formed to use the 90 Elephant or Ferdinand heavy self-propelled guns in early 1943, they used them in action on the northern wing of the Kursk Offensive. They suffered heavy losses because the vehicles lacked a hull machine gun to counter close-quarter infantry attacks. The remaining Elephants were withdrawn to Italy and fought at Anzio. Others were then sent back to the Eastern

Front. The 653rd Battalion was re-equipped with the monster Jagdtigers in time for the Ardennes Offensive. Two other Jagdtiger battalions were formed in early 1945 and they fought in the West until the end of the war.

TIGER ELITE

On every World War II battle front Germany's Tiger tanks proved to be formidable opponents. Allied tank crews rightly feared these monster tanks whenever they appeared. A heavy price was always paid to put them out of action. Not only were they technologically superior to anything the Allies produced, but their crews were always professional and very determined opponents. The German Army's Tiger battalions were always at the centre of the action, driving all before them or dying in the process. Though only just over 1500 Tiger Is were built in total, such was the reputation that this armoured fighting vehicle established during the war that it has become the most famous tanks in the whole of military history.

CHAPTER 8

Rudel's Stukas

When World War II broke out in September 1939, the Junkers Ju 87 Stuka dive-bomber was obsolete. However, during the Blitzkrieg campaigns in Europe between 1939 and 1942 it established itself as a weapon that struck fear into the hearts of enemy soldiers and civilians alike. Even when the tide of war turned against Germany after 1943, the Stuka continued to take to the skies in an anti-tank role. The most famous Stuka pilot was Hans-Ulrich Rudel, whose bravery established him as one of the Luftwaffe's greatest airmen.

One of the enduring images of the German Blitzkrieg is of swarms of dive-bomber aircraft swooping down on hapless Allied columns. The ultimate dive-bomber was the Junkers Ju 87 Sturzkampfflugzeug, or Stuka. Not surprisingly, the name took on a life of its own and entered popular culture.

The dive-bomber was a purpose-built aircraft, designed to drop bombs with pinpoint accuracy on frontline battlefield targets. To support their panzer offensives, the Germans developed close air support into an art form and the Stuka was central to this effort. The secret of German successes in this field was the close integration between air and ground units. Stuka squadrons worked hand-in-hand with ground units so they could intervene rapidly at the decisive point of the battlefield. These highly specialist squadrons were in the thick of the action and developed an impressive reputation. The need to fly deep into the heart of battle meant Stuka pilots suffered some of the highest casualty rates in the Luftwaffe, and as a consequence became some of

As a dive-bomber the Ju 87 was designed originally to carry only three machine guns: one in each wing and a third in the rear cockpit. This woefully inadequate defence, combined with a slow speed, made it very vulnerable to enemy fighters.

the most highly decorated German servicemen. Hans-Ulrich Rudel was the most famous Stuka pilot and squadron commander of the war. He was also the most highly decorated German soldier of the war, being the only serviceman to receive the Knight's Cross with Golden Oak Leaves with Swords and Diamonds.

THE STUKA

Experience with close air support during World War I led many German officers in the newly formed Luftwaffe in the 1930s to develop plans to build a specialist aircraft for this key role. The result was the Junkers Ju 87 Stuka, which first flew in 1935. Although progressively upgraded, the Stuka retained its distinctive gull-winged silhouette that became famous in the early years of World War II.

The single-engined Stuka was fitted with a specialized bomb sight to enable the aircraft to dive vertically on its target, and to automatically open air brakes after bomb release to allow the aircraft to safely pull up when it was 450m (1470ft) from the ground. As a result of this device, the Stuka could drop its bombs within 100m (330ft) of its intended target, and a good pilot could drop his bombs within 10m (32ft). Two

The Ju 87 Stuka first saw operational service with the Condor Legion – a small flight of three aircraft arriving in Spain in December 1937.

wing-mounted 7.92mm machine guns allowed the Stuka to return after dive-bombing runs to strafe their targets. The normal Stuka bomb load was a 1000kg (2200lb) bomb under the fuselage or a 500kg (1100lb) bomb under the fuselage and four 50kg (110lb) bombs under the wings.

To complement this capability the Stukas were fitted with sirens, so-called "Jericho Trumpets", which produced a frightening whine. This, coupled with its vulture-like appearance, made being on the receiving end of a Stuka attack a terrifying experience.

If the Stuka had shortcomings it was in its short range, only 448km (227 miles) in normal close air support operations, and poor air-to-air capabilities. Whenever Stukas came up against determined fighter resistance they were at a distinct disadvantage, and were dependent on the Luftwaffe maintaining air supremacy to allow them to operate freely.

When the war began, just over 330 Stukas had been built and it remained in production until late in 1944, with some 5000 being built in 15 different versions.

From 1942, the Germans began to find themselves faced by huge Soviet tank formations made up of hundreds of T-34s. These were difficult to destroy with traditional dive bombing techniques, so work began to provide the Stuka with more accurate weaponry. The result was the Ju 87G-1, which sported two 37mm high-velocity cannons mounted in underwing pods. These could punch through the armour of any Soviet tank in service, and allowed Stuka squadrons to directly engage the massed tank waves used by the Red Army. It was with this version of the Stuka that Rudel became famously associated. The Germans also developed an early version of what are now known as cluster bombs to counter the large Soviet tank formations. The 500kg (1100lb) SD-4-H1 contained 78 hollow-charge submunitions that could penetrate the thin roof armour of even the heaviest Soviet tank, including the heavily armoured Josef Stalin II.

German close air support tactics were first put into practice during the Spanish Civil War (1936–39), when the first generation of Luftwaffe pilots had a chance to experience modern combat. While the Stuka's

Above: Hans-Ulrich Rudel, Stuka ace and one of the Luftwaffe's most highly decorated combat pilots. He spent his entire career flying Stukas in combat operations but survived the war.

Below: Stukas assembled in northern France in preparation for the assault on England, August 1940

The Allied fleet under air attack in Suda Bay, Crete, late May 1941. During operations in support of the German airborne invasion, Stukas were credited with sinking the Royal Navy cruiser HMS *Gloucester* and a number of destroyers.

top speed of 400kph (250mph) compared poorly to the 574kph (359mph) of the Messerschmitt Bf 109, the Luftwaffe's top-line fighter, this was far from a disadvantage in the close air support role. Too much speed would have reduced the time Stuka pilots had to find their targets. The loitering presence of a Stuka squadron hunting for its targets and then swooping down, could be very terrifying for those on the receiving end of such an attack.

In Spain, Stuka pilots learned that the key to providing successful close air support was having good communications with friendly ground troops, who could pinpoint enemy positions and then direct air strikes against them. Combat experience in Poland and France later reinforced this and confirmed the validity of Stuka tactics. This saved the Stukas valuable time finding targets and also ensured that only targets that would influence the ground battle were engaged. So-called *Stukaleiters*, or Stuka controllers, were posted to each panzer division by the Luftwaffe. These men were usually serving Stuka pilots from the squadrons assigned to that sector of the front, to bind together the Stukas and panzers into a single force. *Stukaleiters* were given armoured halftracks to work in so they could keep up with the panzer commanders and had air-to-ground radios so they could talk-in attack aircraft to their targets. The Stukas have been described as the panzers' "flying artillery", but they brought more to the Blitzkrieg than just firepower. The Stukas ranged far ahead over hostile territory and provided German ground forces with early warning of troop strengths, movements and terrain obstacles.

While the Stukas reigned supreme in the Blitzkrieg battles of 1939 and 1940, when Luftwaffe chief Hermann Goering sent them into action against British airfields during the Battle of Britain the thin German fighter cover available meant they suffered heavy losses.

Over the Mediterranean in 1941 the Stuka came into its own as an anti-ship weapon. Luftwaffe air superiority meant Royal Navy warships could be attacked without interruption by Stuka squadrons flying from Italian and Greek air bases. The Stuka's dive-bomber systems proved highly effective against British warships, revisiting the successes enjoyed during the Dunkirk evacuation in 1940, when almost 250 Allied ships had been lost to German air power. The high point of the Stuka campaign in the Mediterranean theatre was the support for the airborne invasion of Crete in May 1941. After blasting open the Allied defences for the German paratroopers, who lacked tank or artillery support, the Stukas turned their attention to the Royal Navy warships sent to evacuate the defenders. Nine British warships went to the bottom and 15 were heavily damaged after becoming victims of dive-bombing.

The most famous Stuka pilot of the war did not begin his career at all auspiciously. In 1938, Hans-Ulrich Rudel was posted to one of the first Stuka squadrons, but was a slow learner, and far from popular with his peers because he did not join in the boisterous mess life typical of

Ju 87s over the Western Desert operating against British and Commonwealth forces. Stukas were first sent to North Africa in December 1941, and free from Allied fighters proved effective in raids on Tobruk and Bir Hakim in 1942.

the prewar Luftwaffe. The 32-year-old Rudel was a teetotaller who did not smoke and spent all his time when not flying playing sport. A few months later he was shipped out to be trained as a reconnaissance pilot. After flying reconnaissance missions during the Polish campaign, he pressed to be transferred back to Stukas. His wish was granted, but it meant he missed the French campaign because he was undergoing flight training. Rudel was now assigned to perhaps the most famous Stuka wing of the war, Stuka Group 2 (SG) *Immelmann*, named after the famous World War I fighter ace. An argument with his commanding officer resulted in Rudel being grounded during the Greek and Crete campaigns, and being employed instead as a maintenance officer.

RUDEL ON THE EASTERN FRONT

Rudel was determined to get into the action, and eventually a friend who commanded one of the wing's squadrons relented, allowing him to fly as his wingman between his maintenance work on the flight line. He flew on the first day of the invasion of Russia and was in action on almost every day for the remainder of the war, except when he was in hospital or receiving medals from his Führer. The wing was in the thick of the action on the central sector of the Eastern Front, supporting panzer columns heading towards Smolensk and Moscow. Rudel became renowned for his determination to press home his dive-bombing runs, pulling up only at the very last minute to ensure his bombs landed on target.

In August 1941, Rudel's wing was transferred to the Leningrad Front where German troops were besieging the cradle of the Soviet revolution. With Germans on the outskirts of the city, several Soviet Navy ships trapped in the Gulf of Finland regularly turned their big guns on their enemies. The *Immelmann* wing was given the task of knocking out the warships. Its main target was the 26,416-tonne (26,000-ton) battleship *Marat*. The wing's first attack on 21 September with 500kg (1100lb) bombs failed to penetrate the warship's armour, in spite of Rudel putting a bomb square on target after flying through an anti-aircraft barrage thrown up by 1000 guns.

When 1000kg (2200lb) bombs arrived at the wing, Rudel led a new attack on the *Marat*. He pressed home the attack with his typical determination and only released his bomb 300m (980ft) above the target. Rudel's bomb penetrated the warship's magazine. As it exploded in a massive fireball, Rudel struggled to regain control of his aircraft after blacking out, and only managed to pull it up 4m (12ft) from the sea. If that was not enough of a problem, three Soviet fighters now jumped the Stukas. The attack won Rudel the Knight's Cross.

The Soviet winter offensive of 1941–42 saw the *Immelmann* wing supporting hard-pressed German defences in central Russia. When a Soviet tank column broke through the front and threatened the wing's airfield, Rudel led air strikes that drove them back. For three days, the

Stukas kept the Soviets at bay until the Waffen-SS *Das Reich* Division arrived to relieve the situation. By now Rudel had notched up more than 500 missions and was posted home to train a new Stuka squadron. Not wanting to be out of the action, he soon managed to pull a few strings and got his squadron transferred to southern Russia, where the Germans were pushing south to seize Stalin's Caucasus oil wells. In the middle of the battle for Stalingrad, Rudel was diagnosed with jaundice but after spending a few days in a field hospital, he absented himself, returned to the front and took command of a squadron of the *Immelmann* wing. These were desperate days for the Luftwaffe in southern Russia. As Soviet tanks moved to surround the German Sixth Army in Stalingrad, units such as Rudel's Stukas were needed to hold back the Red Army. The Soviet advance was rolling up one German airfield after another, making it more difficult for the short-range Stukas to help the trapped German soldiers.

The cannon-armed Ju 87G-1 was designed specifically as an anti-tank weapon, its two 37mm Flak 18 cannon firing tungsten-cored shells. Rudel took part in trials of the G-1 in late 1942, and flew the aircraft for the first time operationally in the Crimea in May 1943.

CANNON BIRDS

Rudel was now recalled to Germany to form the first experimental anti-tank Stuka unit equipped with the 37mm cannon-armed Ju 87s, dubbed "Cannon Birds" by their crews. Rudel took the unit to the Crimea to help counter a Soviet amphibious landing on the Kuban peninsula. The Cannon Birds proved to be an outstanding success against Soviet landing craft bringing troops and supplies ashore, with Rudel alone claiming 70 destroyed. Personally awarded the Oak Leaves to his Knight's Cross by a grateful Führer for his work in the Kuban, Rudel was now posted back to the *Immelmann* wing in charge of its Ju 87 G-1 anti-tank squadron, in time to lead it during the July 1943 Kursk Offensive.

As expected, his squadron was in the thick of the action supporting II Waffen-SS Panzer Corps as it attacked on the southern axis of Operation Citadel. His Cannon Birds ranged ahead of the panzers, intercepting and destroying Soviet reserve tank columns moving to the front. Scores of tanks were claimed destroyed by Rudel and his wingmen, with the squadron commander alone claiming to have destroyed

12 T-34s on a single day. Experience taught the Stuka pilots to aim for vulnerable parts of the Soviet tanks, such as engine bays and turret roofs. The exhaust smoke of the Soviet tanks proved a useful aiming point for the Stuka gunners, and a hit against the engine often resulted in a catastrophic explosion. The Soviet practice of loading extra fuel drums on the rear of their tanks made them very vulnerable to Stuka cannon fire. To get a good shot at the T-34s, Rudel recommended dropping down to 15m (50ft) to give the Stuka pilot a good look at the target. Here the slow speed of the Stuka came into its own, because it gave the pilot plenty of time to lay his guns on target.

These attacks proved devastating to the morale of Soviet tank columns and the infantry who rode into the battle on the rear decks of the T-34s. To counter the Stuka threat the Soviets started to move anti-aircraft guns close to their tank columns. In turn, Rudel began to have

Stukas on the Eastern Front flying close air support over an SdKfz 250 ground-to-air communications halftrack. Such mobile radio links were vital for the efficient and safe deployment of ground-attack aircraft on the frontline.

a pair of bomb- and machine-gun-armed Stukas circling overhead as his Cannon Birds lined up for their attacks. The supporting Stukas would strafe and bomb Soviet anti-aircraft batteries that attempted to open fire. They also provided early warning of the appearance of Soviet fighters that were starting to challenge German air superiority on the Eastern Front. In spite of this covering fire, Rudel's aircraft routinely returned to base full of bullet holes.

After Hitler's Kursk Offensive stalled, the Soviets immediately opened a huge offensive against the northern wing of the German forces around Orel, opening a huge breach in the front. Rudel's tank-killing Stukas were rushed northwards to help stabilize the situation and give ground reinforcements time to mobilize. In the midst of this chaos, Rudel's aircraft was badly shot up, but he managed to make a forced landing behind German lines and return to the fray. Soviet offensives continued to require the close attention of the *Immelmann* wing, and Rudel was appointed to command its 3rd Group after his predecessor was killed in action. He had now flown some 1500 sorties and personally destroyed 60 Soviet tanks, earning him the Oak Leaves and Swords to his Knight's Cross.

Time after time, his Stukas saved the day during the Soviet winter offensive in the Ukraine, culminating in a decisive intervention during the Battle of Kirovograd in November 1943, when Rudel and his pilots blunted an attack by hundreds of T-34s. By now Rudel and his Stuka pilots had been turned into national heroes, featuring almost daily in Nazi propaganda broadcasts announcing more tank kills, desperate situations saved and medals won. To the ordinary German soldiers,

Rudel's tank-killing Stukas were known as the "front fire brigade" because they were always called on to dampen down the most combustible sections of the front. While other Stuka units had switched to flying the two-engine Henschel Hs 129 armed with a 75mm cannon, or ground-attack versions of the Focke-Wulf Fw 190, Rudel stuck with his trusty Ju 87. Rudel's squadron operated from rudimentary forward air strips, and his leadership was instrumental in keeping his ground crews working in freezing weather to put damaged aircraft back in the air time and time again, with minimal spares, tools and facilities. Once in the air, Rudel's pilots followed him into attack after attack. He appeared fearless. Even when shot down over enemy territory, he somehow managed to escape and return to the cockpit of a Stuka. This

A flight of Ju 87Ds over the River Dnieper, Russia, 1943. The Ju 87D was one of the most heavily armed Stukas to see service – it could carry a bomb load of up to 1800kg (4000lb) or weapon pods under each wing, each with six machine guns and two 20mm cannon.

incident followed a successful attack to destroy a bridge over the River Dnieper in March 1944. Twenty Soviet fighters swooped on his squadron, forcing one of Rudel's pilots to land in territory held by the Red Army. Rudel landed to try to pick up his man, only to have his aircraft get stuck in mud. Russian soldiers captured Rudel and his two comrades. He swam a river and walked 50km (31 miles) in an escape bid. Two days later, he reached German lines and was soon back in the air.

Tank killing with the G-1 model Stuka became a Rudel speciality, and by August 1944 he claimed his 320th tank kill. The collapse of the German Army Group Centre in July 1944 brought the *Immelmann* wing northwards to the Courland peninsula, where it was thrown into one desperate battle after another. In October Rudel was promoted lieutenant-colonel and given command of his beloved *Immelmann* wing. There was little time to bask in the glory, and he had to lead his fliers to Hungary to help Waffen-SS panzer divisions blast a corridor through to 100,000 German troops besieged in Budapest. Soviet fighters were now swarming over the Eastern Front, making it highly dangerous for the lumbering Cannon Birds to go into action. In the space of a few days Rudel was shot down twice, but returned to the cockpit of a Stuka with his leg in a plaster cast. With more than 2400 missions in his log book and 463 tank kills claimed, Hitler made him the only recipient of the Knight's Cross with Golden Oak Leaves with Swords and Diamonds in January 1945. Hitler tried to ground Germany's most highly decorated soldier, but Rudel insisted on returning to combat duty leading his wing.

Russian tanks were now advancing into Silesia, and Rudel's wing was transferred to try to contain the situation. Flying from German soil, Rudel's Stukas were able to rescue several German units cut off trying

A Ju 87D being armed for a bombing sortie over northern Russia during the winter of 1943–44. Stukas first saw service in this region over Leningrad at the end of 1941.

to retreat westwards to safety. When the Soviets pushed a bridgehead over the River Oder in February 1945, Rudel threw his Stukas into action. He alone destroyed four Soviet tanks, before having an aircraft shot out from under him. After struggling back to base, Rudel took off again to continue knocking out more than a dozen Josef Stalin tanks. In the midst of another attack run his aircraft was blown apart by Soviet flak. Rudel woke up in a field hospital to find out his left leg had been amputated. Despite being told his flying days were finished, Germany's top Stuka pilot had other ideas. Only six weeks later he was back flying from bases in Czechoslovakia. When Germany surrendered in May, he led the remnants of his *Immelmann* wing on a last flight to American-controlled airfields in southern Germany.

The USAF's A-10 Thunderbolt II, a ground-attack, anti-tank aircraft directly inspired by Rudel's success with the Ju 87G-1. The A-10 is built around a massive seven-barrelled 30mm gun capable of firing 4200 armour-piercing rounds per minute.

TANK KILLERS

Rudel was instrumental in developing the tactics of using cannon-armed aircraft in the anti-tank role. The exploits of his Stukas during the Battle of Kursk was the inspiration used by the United States Air Force in designing the A-10 Warthog tank-busting aircraft at the height of the Cold War, when there was a requirement to counter massed divisions of Soviet tanks in central Europe. This aircraft was built around a multi-barrelled cannon specifically to counter enemy tanks.

As a leader of warriors, Rudel was unsurpassed. He led from the front and set a pace that few could equal. In the course of 2530 missions, Rudel personally destroyed 517 Soviet tanks – the equivalent of five Soviet tank corps. This was on top of a battleship, cruiser, 70 landing craft, 800 trucks, 150 artillery pieces, as well as numerous bunkers, bridges and supply dumps. He also managed to achieve nine confirmed air-to-air kills. Perhaps more striking was the fact that Rudel was shot down 30 times by ground fire, and wounded five times. On top of this, he successfully rescued six of his pilots who had been shot down behind enemy lines. This was the mark of the man, who ranked leading his men into battle as the highest duty of any soldier.

CHAPTER 9

Hitler's Foreign Legion: The SS Volunteers

While many brave non-German men and women across Europe took up arms against their new Nazi rulers after 1939, others decided to join the cause of the Third Reich. More than 25 of the 39 Waffen-SS divisions raised during World War II contained a significant foreign element. The best units were those from Scandinavia and western Europe, the *Wiking* Division standing out as a truly elite formation on a par with the other Waffen-SS panzer divisions.

A t its peak in the autumn of 1942, Hitler's empire stretched from the Arctic circle to North Africa, and the Atlantic coast of France to the Caucasus mountains in Russia. As the war raged across Europe hundreds of thousands of Hitler's subjects threw in their lot with the Führer's "New Order". These men were dubbed "collaborators" for their treachery and so became some of Hitler's most enthusiastic supporters. For them, there was no going back.

In a bizarre twist of fate, many of these men ended up in the Waffen-SS, an organization founded on Nazi racial purity theory. Bosnian Muslims, Albanians, Hungarians, Ukranians and even Russians – all "untermenschen" or sub-humans according to Hitler's crazy policy of racial characteristics – ended up wearing the ultimate symbol of the Führer's master race, the Nordic runes of the SS.

During the 1930s Hitler insisted on the highest physical standards for SS recruits, as well as demanding they be "racially pure". Would-be SS recruits had to prove they were not tainted with "non-Aryan" blood.

A Norwegian volunteer to the Waffen-SS. The first SS unit of foreigners was the Standarte *Nordland* made up of Danes and Norwegians, formed in 1940. It was joined the same year by the Standarte *Westland* of Dutch and Belgians.

Heinrich Himmler, Reichsführer-SS, saw the opportunity of exploiting the vast reserves of manpower available in the occupied territories after 1940, and began recruiting national units for an anti-communist war.

They also had to be fanatical Nazis. Only volunteers were accepted. Not surprisingly, recruitment to the SS was a slow business in the run-up to World War II. Hitler initially moved carefully in his plans to create the Waffen-SS – or armed SS – as the Nazi Party's private army prior to the outbreak of war to avoid antagonizing German Army chiefs. The SS became locked in a bureaucratic battle with the Army High Command over the allocation of manpower. A special dispensation was needed to exempt SS volunteers from their legal obligation to complete military service in the army.

Heinrich Himmler, the head of the SS, was determined to find a way around the objections of the Army to an expansion of the Waffen-SS, but it was not until the occupation of Czechoslovakia in 1938 that he had access to a source of manpower out of the grip of the generals. The so-called "ethnic Germans", or *Volksdeutsche*, who lived in Czechoslovakia were not officially citizens of the German Reich, and were therefore not liable for conscription into the army. These were the first "foreign" recruits into the Waffen-SS, although they served alongside German volunteers in the early units of Himmler's elite force. At this time Himmler was considering grouping the *Volksdeutsche* in their own units. The conquests of Poland, Denmark, Norway, Holland, Belgium, France, Yugoslavia and Greece soon followed, bringing in more potential recruits within range of Himmler's recruiting teams, and opening the door for the formation of the first "foreign" SS units.

As Hitler ordered the expansion of the Waffen-SS in the summer of 1940, the first foreign units were formed from Belgian, Danish,

Norwegian and Dutch recruits. Himmler's racial purity requirements could be fudged because of the alleged "kindred stock" of these nationalities. These men were either prewar fascists or opportunists who wanted to show their allegiance to the New Order in Europe.

The recruits from the Low Countries were formed into the *Westland* Standarte (Regiment), while the Scandinavians were assigned to the *Nordland* Regiment. They were eventually linked in December 1940 with the *Germania* Standarte to form the nucleus of the Waffen-SS *Wiking* 5th Motorized Division. Its commander for the next three years was Felix Steiner, who was one of the more talented Waffen-SS divisional commanders.

The division's first campaign was the invasion of Russia in June 1941, and it spent the next four years fighting exclusively on the Eastern Front. The *Wiking* Division soon established a reputation as a hard-fighting outfit during the breakneck advance into the Ukraine. It was decimated during heavy defensive fighting along the Mius Front in the southern sector during the winter of 1941–42, but was rebuilt in time for the German summer offensive into the Caucasus, including the addition to its strength of a panzer battalion to boost its offensive punch. The division pushed southwards, capturing the key Mozdok oil wells, before the Soviet offensive that trapped the German Sixth Army

A Panther tank of the *Wiking* Motorized Division. This unit of "kindred stock" from western Europe was granted divisional status in late 1940, and as a representative of the new fascist order took part in the invasion of Russia in June 1941.

at Stalingrad forced Hitler's troops to pull out of the Caucasus. Several more months of bitter fighting in the Ukraine followed, as the *Wiking* troops first held back a new Soviet offensive preparing the way for the Germans' next counterstroke. The attack of the division at Krasnoarmeyskoye in February 1943 smashed open the Soviet front and opened the way for the recapture of Kharkov. Although held in reserve during the Kursk Offensive in July, the division was thrown into the thick of the action in a doomed bid to hold back the Soviet summer and autumn offensive that liberated the eastern Ukraine. It was committed to action during August 1943, alongside the Waffen-SS *Totenkopf* and *Das Reich* Divisions, to try to seal a huge breach in the German front. In a month of swirling tank battles, the *Wiking* Division destroyed hundreds of Soviet T-34s, but was eventually forced to retreat towards Kiev. It was pulled out of the line in October to be reorganized as a full Waffen-SS panzer division, under its new commander Herbert Gille, before being committed to the defence of the Dnieper bend.

The desperate battles along the River Dnieper saw the division fight its most famous action when it was surrounded in the Korsun-Cherkassy Pocket in February 1944. After being trapped for several days it broke out, losing thousands of men and all its heavy equipment in the process. Even then the desperate men of the division were thrown straight back

Himmler reviews an anti-tank unit of an SS *freiwilligen* (volunteer) infantry division in 1944. These *freiwilligen* units originated from pro-Nazi legions recruited in western Europe that were sponsored by the SS. They were never considered part of the SS organization.

into the line as an ad hoc battlegroup to hold the line at Kowel in the face of another Soviet offensive. Eventually it was re-equipped and replenished, with more Nordic recruits and Panther tanks, in time to hold back the Soviets from Warsaw in the autumn of 1944. Its final battles were fought in Hungary, when it had some success spearheading Hitler's doomed offensive to free German troops trapped in Budapest.

Himmler's lust to expand the Waffen-SS was not quenched by the formation of the *Wiking* Division, and he quickly moved to further tap the manpower pool of the occupied territories. He wanted to set up so-called legions recruited from Belgian, Dutch, Norwegian, Danish and Swedish volunteers. A French legion was initially set up under army control, before eventually being transferred to the Waffen-SS. These legions were all closely linked to fascist or right-wing nationalist groups in their countries. Norwegian collaborator Vidkun Quisling's government, for example, was instrumental in recruiting volunteers to the Waffen-SS.

Nazi propaganda touted these foreign legions as part of a pan-European anti-Bolshevik crusade, and they were quickly dispatched to the Eastern Front. Regular heroic newsreel reports recounted their exploits fighting the Red Army, although in the first couple of years of the Russian campaign they were more likely to be found on anti-partisan duty behind the front. Later in the war they would be given more than enough opportunities to die in battle against the Soviets.

The Flemish-speaking Belgian-Dutch Legion was bound together by a common language and hatred of the old Belgian state. A French-speaking Belgian unit formed in 1941 was drawn from the Walloon region of Belgium, under officers who were high-ranking officials in the fascist Rexist party. After serving for three years on quiet sectors of the Eastern

Norwegian volunteers begin initial training under Waffen-SS supervision. Although the rank and file of these volunteer units were foreign nationals, the officers were invariably German and Nazi loyalists.

Front, when the situation in the Ukraine became desperate the unit was transferred to this key sector. In the process, it was expanded into Storm Brigade *Walloon* and then fought side by side with the *Wiking* Division in the Korsun-Cherkassy Pocket. It covered the withdrawal of the *Wiking* as the rearguard. The brigade's exploits earned it the Führer's gratitude and its commander, Rexist leader Leon Degrelle, the Swords and Oak Leaves to his Knight's Cross. The unit was destroyed in the battle for Berlin in 1945, but Degrelle managed to escape to South America. He was one of only three of the original 850 recruits to the brigade who survived the war.

Unlike the *Wiking* Division's foreign standarten who had German officers, the Scandinavian and western European legions were led by commanders from their own countries. This meant their military usefulness was limited at first, and they had to be gently exposed to the violence on the Eastern Front to gain combat experience. The legions were organized as infantry units with light weapons and sometimes StuG III assault guns, and rarely mustered more than 2000 men in the field at any one time. When the legions were eventually expanded into nominal "divisions" to satisfy Himmler's desire to create more and bigger units, they could rarely muster 10,000 men each – half the strength of a German Army or Waffen-SS division.

In 1943 the bulk of the legions were grouped into the Waffen-SS *Nordland* Panzergrenadier Division, which fought tenaciously on the northern sector of the Eastern Front throughout 1944. Its hour of glory came in September 1944, when its timely intervention prevented the encirclement of the Eighteenth Army. The remnants of the division went down fighting around Hitler's bunker in Berlin in April and May 1945.

Eventually some 50,000 Dutch men joined the Waffen-SS, the majority of whom served in the *Landsturm-Nederland* Militia Division, which initially helped to prop up German rule in Holland before being sent to the Eastern Front for the remainder of the war. Belgium provided 40,000 recruits to the Waffen-SS, evenly split between Flemish- and French-speaking volunteers, with most of the Flemish speakers eventually serving in the *Langemark* Waffen-SS Division. More than 20,000 French signed up to Hitler's anti-Bolshevik crusade, while Denmark and Norway each provided 6000 volunteers.

Himmler loved the propaganda value provided by these legions, as he attempted to prove that Europe was united behind the New Order. Two pure propaganda units were the so-called *British Free Corps* and Indian Legion formed from turncoat prisoners of war. They never went into battle except in newsreel films.

When German armies rolled east in June 1941, they swiftly conquered the Baltic states of Estonia, Latvia and Lithuania, where they were greeted as "liberators". In 1939, as a result of the Soviet-German non-aggression pact that had paved the way for Hitler's conquest of

Above: Many ethnic groups, like these Cossacks, were willing to fight with the Nazis in the hope of achieving national self-determination in some unseen future and because they hated the Russians.

Opposite above: A member of the 7th SS Freiwilligen Gebirgs (Mountain) Division *Prinz Eugen*. This division was formed in 1942 and comprised ethnic Germans (*Volksdeutsche*) from the Balkan region.

Opposite below: After the invasion of Russia the Nazis also exploited disaffected nationalities from within the Soviet Union. The SS took recruits from among Byelorussians, Turkestanis, Ukrainians and from the Baltic States.

Poland, Stalin was able to freely send in his troops to forcibly incorporate the three countries into the Soviet Union.

Volunteers flocked to join police and militia units being set up by their new German rulers and soon Himmler started to take a close interest in the Latvian and Estonian units, and incorporated several into the Waffen-SS. He was particularly impressed by their zeal in helping SS Einsatzgruppen killing squads murder Jews in ghettos that were being set up in the region. Thanks to the ethnic affinity of the Estonians and Latvians with Scandinavia, Himmler was willing to smooth their way into the Waffen-SS. The Catholic Lithuanians were beyond the pale as Slavs as far as Himmler was concerned, so they languished in special police battalions.

Baltic units were highly prized by German commanders for their expertise in counter-partisan units. Eventually, they were to be formed into three Waffen-SS divisions. When German troops were trapped in the Baltic states in 1944, the Latvian and Estonian units fought on even after Germany surrendered the following year. Many took to the woods as partisans against the Soviets and continued fighting into the 1950s.

According to Nazi racial classification there were more than 2.5 million ethnic Germans, or *Volksdeutsche*, spread around eastern Europe. Himmler quickly set about resettling them in areas forcibly emptied of Jews and Slavs. They were also recruited in large numbers into the Waffen-SS. Early in the war they were used to provide man-

power for mainstream Waffen-SS units, but in 1942 the first *Volksdeutsche* unit was formed. The 7th Mountain *Prinz Eugen* Division drew its *Volksdeutsche* recruits from Hungary, Romania and Yugoslavia. It was predominately engaged in counter-insurgency operations against Tito's partisans in Yugoslavia for the remainder of the war, gaining a fearsome reputation as one of the most reliable and effective units in this confused and brutal war zone. In 1944 it was reinforced with drafts from the disbanded Albanian Waffen-SS unit.

The 18th *Horst Wessel* Panzergrenadier Division was formed from *Volksdeutsche* recruits in Hungary during the spring of 1944, before being sent to fight on the central sector of the Eastern Front. Czech *Volksdeutsche* formed the bulk of the recruits to the *Bohmen-Mahren* Division, which first fought in the Balkans and Hungary before ending the war in its homeland.

In spite of Nazi ideology that stressed German racial superiority over Slavs, by 1943 Himmler was getting increasingly desperate for manpower to fill out his expanding phalanx of Waffen-SS units, and started to turn to eastern Europe for recruits. An innovator along these lines was SS-General Erich von dem Bach-Zelewski, who recruited the first units of ex-Soviet prisoners of war into the Waffen-SS in 1943 to fight partisans in central Russia. The so-called *Kaminski* Brigade blazed a trail of terror throughout German-

Above: Some trusted foreign units had their own senior officers, such as General Vlasov of the Cossacks. Having betrayed Stalin, there was no hope for these men but a German victory.

Opposite above: The Nazis became adept at exploiting racial, ethnic and religious difference for their own ends. This was particularly the case in the Balkans, where Muslims (as here) were organized to fight the Christian Serb partisans.

Opposite below: Himmler even recruited the help of the Grand Mufti of Jerusalem (in white hat) to encourage Muslim troops in their loyalty to the New Order.

occupied Russia for almost a year, killing thousands of civilians in reprisals for partisan attacks, until its commander went too far – even for the SS – during the Warsaw uprising, and was executed on Bach-Zelewski's orders.

A far more impressive unit was the 14th Galician Division which was recruited from Catholic Ukrainians in 1943. It was almost destroyed in the Brody-Tarnow Pocket during the summer of 1944, when only 3000 out of 14,000 men managed to break out of the Soviet encirclement. It eventually fought in Hungary and Austria, where it surrendered to British troops. The intervention of the Vatican saved the remnants of the division being handed over to the Soviets, unlike other units composed of turncoat Soviet citizens.

As defeat after defeat rolled back the Eastern Front in 1944, Himmler at last decided to turn the surviving two million Russian prisoners of war held by the Germans into an anti-Soviet army. After spending three years trying to work these men to death in slave labour camps, this was an amazing change of heart. Three million Soviet prisoners had already died from neglect and they were becoming increasingly desperate. The approaching Red Army offered little prospect of liberation to captured Russian soldiers, whom Stalin had already declared to be "traitors".

The former Red Army general Andrei Vlasov was persuaded to tour prison camps to recruit men for the Waffen-SS Russian army. He eventually raised two divisions, and they briefly saw action on the Eastern Front in the final months of the war. They retreated to Prague and then turned on the German garrison in the city to help Czech resistance fighters that had risen in revolt. The change of heart did not do them any good, and the US Army eventually handed them over to the Soviets after the war, with the result that the majority were executed.

Contrary to popular legend, the Waffen-SS did not recruit Don Cossacks. These were part of the German Army, although they did fight alongside Waffen-SS units in the Balkans.

BALKAN DIVISIONS

In spite of being able to overrun Yugoslav in a matter of weeks in April 1941, the Germans were never able to subdue the country's population. Tito's communist partisans were soon causing problems and, by 1944, 20 German divisions containing 700,000 troops were tied down fighting a guerrilla war. Rather than divert German soldiers from the frontline for this task, it was decided to recruit locals to fight against Tito to capitalize on the region's age-old ethnic and religious hatreds. As the war progressed, the need to increase recruitment to these units became critical.

Eventually two divisions of Muslim soldiers were recruited from the region, which is today known as Bosnia, but under German rule was part of the Croatian Nazi puppet state. Himmler tried to make the units of the 13th *Handschar* and 23rd *Kama* Divisions follow the traditions of the old Muslim units of the Hapsburg Empire, which had ruled the

region before World War I. Former Hapsburg officers were recruited to lead these new units. Ethnic Albanian Muslims were also recruited in 1944 into their own division, the 21st *Skanderbeg*, named after the national hero of the Albanians. In a bid to use these Muslim divisions to undermine British rule in the Middle East, Himmler drafted the Grand Mufti of Jerusalem to oversee these units' religious practices. If anything, this shows the depth to which Himmler had sunk to fill out his Waffen-SS divisions.

They proved useful in the partisan operations, but when faced by determined troops were less effective. The Muslim units were motivated by a desire to fight their Christian Serb neighbours, who formed the core support for Tito's partisans, although the war in Yugoslavia was characterized by shifting allegiances. The Albanians, in particular, gained a gruesome reputation for committing atrocities. Attempts to move the *Skanderbeg* Division away from Yugoslavia in 1944 to fight in the West were a disaster, ending in a mutiny. The unit was eventually disbanded.

Splits in the partisan movement led to some Serb supporters of the old Royalist regime in Belgrade to switch allegiances to the Germans. The Serbian Volunteer Corps was transferred to the Waffen-SS in 1944.

Four divisions of Hungarians were recruited from supporters of the Arrow Cross Nazi movement in late 1944 as Soviet troops invaded their country. These units were all destroyed in the fighting in early 1945.

The formation of Benito Mussolini's rump fascist republic in northern Italy provided the recruiting ground for two of the final Waffen-SS divisions to be raised during the war. They existed for only a few months before disintegrating in the German rout in Italy in April 1945.

Dutch members of the SS await their fate behind Allied barbed wire. After the collapse of the Nazi regime in 1945, men such as these faced a very uncertain future. Branded as traitors, collaborators and, as members of the SS, criminals, all they could do was await judgment.

Skorzeny's Commandos

Otto Skorzeny was the nearest thing the Third Reich ever had to a swashbuckling war hero. A young Austrian who joined the Nazi Party in 1930, he led some of most daring missions of the war. He rescued the Italian dictator Benito Mussolini from captivity in 1943, headed up SS special forces, seized the Hungarian Government and then organized squads of American-speaking commandos to operate behind US lines during the Battle of the Bulge.

A t only 35 years of age, Otto Skorzeny was placed in charge of all SS special forces units and soon gained the confidence of Hitler, who treated him as his personal "Mr Fixit" during the final two years of the war. Skorzeny was a classic "chancer" and his daring antics appealed to Hitler's sense of the melodramatic. For the head of the Reich's "secret" special forces units, Skorzeny had a remarkably high public profile. The Nazi propaganda machine went into overdrive whenever he staged some dramatic operation. The Führer dubbed him "the most dangerous man in Europe" and liked the idea that Allied leaders could not sleep easily for fear of falling victim to Skorzeny's raiders.

His rise to prominence owed much to the politics of the Führer's "court". SS leaders were keen to build up their own covert forces to rival the famous *Brandenburg* Division that was the "direct action" arm of Admiral Wilhelm Canaris, the chief of the German Army High Command's counter-intelligence organization, which became famous as the Abwehr.

Otto Skorzeny became involved with special operations in 1943 after serving with the *Das Reich* and *Leibstandarte* Divisions. His exploits made him famous as Hitler's own commando and a soldier who got things done.

The *Brandenburg* Division saw action on all fronts during the Blitzkrieg advances of 1939–42, operating behind enemy lines, often wearing foreign uniforms to gain surprise. To the paranoid leaders of the SS, Canaris was just as much an enemy as the Americans, British or Soviets. His Abwehr was seen as a nest of traitors by SS leaders, such as Heinrich Himmler and Ernst Kaltenbrunner, who suspected Canaris of opening secret talks with the Allies and supporting anti-Nazi groups in Germany. The *Brandenburgers* were, in turn, suspected of being a "Trojan Horse" that could be used by Canaris against the Nazi regime.

To rival the Abwehr, the SS set up its own intelligence service, the Sicherheitsdienst (SD) headed by the sinister Reinhard Heydrich, and then the Reich Main Security Office (RHSA) was formed as Germany's internal security organization. It had responsibility for the feared Geheimstaatspolizei, or Gestapo. The SD had already gained experience with special forces during the conquests of Austria and Czechoslovakia. They then provided agent provocateur units in Poland, who provided a convenient excuse for Hitler's September 1939 invasion. The SD agents faked an attack on a Polish border post, and even executed a concentration camp inmate dressed in a Polish uniform to provide a body and complete the fiction that Warsaw's troops had provoked Hitler into attacking.

After Czech commandos, trained by the British Special Operations Executive (SOE), assassinated Heydrich in 1942, SS and Abwehr rivalry reached new levels of intensity. A department for "special troops", Amt

Above: A DFS 230 glider on a mountainside close to Mussolini's prison at Gran Sasso. Though Skorzeny took the glory for the rescue, it was the Luftwaffe that supplied the gliders and most of the men.

Opposite above: Some of Skorzeny's men after the successful assault on the Gran Sasso Hotel. Though wearing Fallschirmjäger kit, Skorzeny's team were in fact all members of the Waffen-SS.

Opposite below: Skorzeny's rescue of Mussolini from the Gran Sasso Hotel (seen here) on 12 September 1943 was a political coup ordered personally by Hitler. The Italian Government had surrendered to the Allies on the 3rd, and the Salerno landings had begun on the 9th. Hitler needed Mussolini to head a new fascist regime in Italy.

VI-S, was set up under Ernst Kaltenbrunner's RHSA to control SS special forces units. Skorzeny was the man chosen to lead this organization. The 1.95m (6ft 6in) tall Austrian had joined the Nazi Party even before Hitler rose to power. In the aftermath of the Austrian *Anschluss* in 1938, Skorzeny had come to the notice of Nazi chiefs when he played a prominent part in thwarting a counter-coup by Austrians opposed to the German occupation. After seeing service in the *Das Reich* Division during the invasions of Yugoslavia and Russia, he gained a reputation as a daredevil officer, but after he was injured in December 1941 he was put on light duties at the *Leibstandarte*'s depot. On 20 April 1943, Skorzeny was promoted to Waffen-SS captain and given command of Amt VI-S.

Benito Mussolini immediately after his rescue on his way to the Storch aircraft that would fly him to Rome. The Italian officer on his left is his former gaoler

His new command was little more than an office. The Abwehr had successfully frustrated previous attempts to create SS special forces. Skorzeny moved into Friedenthal castle near Oranienburg and set up a training camp for the Jagdverbande (Hunting Group) 502, which was to be trained for a wide range of sabotage and subversion missions. This force became known as the Friedenthal Organization. Skorzeny was obsessed by the British commandos, who since 1941 had been staging raids into Hitler's Fortress Europe. He collected captured commando weapons, silenced Sten guns, demolition explosives and the like. The SS was in the process of forming its own parachute force and Skorzeny was soon given command of this unit, designated the 500th SS Parachute Battalion. Skorzeny also set in train the formation of more jagdverbande units to operate in specific regions. These units mirrored the role and capabilities of the Abwehr's *Brandenburg* regiments, with personnel trained in local languages and supplied with uniforms of foreign armies. Units included an "eastern" battalion trained to operate on the Russian Front, a "southeastern" battalion trained to work in the Balkans, a central European unit and a west European unit. The Luftwaffe wing, Kampfgeschwader (KG) 200, was assigned to work with Skorzeny to fly and parachute his men far behind enemy lines.

There was much talk and training, but Skorzeny's men had little chance to prove themselves until their leader was summoned to Hitler's headquarters in East Prussia on 23 July 1943 for a very special mission.

THE MUSSOLINI RESCUE

Allied landings in Sicily earlier in the month had eventually forced German troops back to the Italian mainland. This subsequently caused the overthrow of the Italian fascist dictator, Benito Mussolini, and the Rome government to seek an armistice with the Allies. The "Duce" was arrested and whisked away into secret custody.

Hitler was determined to rescue his old ally and make an attempt to keep Italy serving the Axis. Luftwaffe Lieutenant-General Kurt Student and his airborne forces were scouring Italy for Mussolini's hiding place, but Hitler wanted to involve the SS in this prestige mission. Skorzeny was sent to Italy to help Student, with the Führer extolling him: "you will succeed". He took 50 of his Friedenthal men with him to Rome.

For several weeks, the Germans searched Italy for their target. Skorzeny used the special powers granted by the Führer to ensure the hunt received the attention demanded by Hitler. He flew in aircraft to reconnoitre remote islands and mountain hideouts and dispatched undercover agents to follow-up "hot" leads. By early September 1943, Skorzeny had narrowed his hunt to a mountain top hotel high in central Italy at Gran Sasso. Student formed a strike force of his paratroopers and planned to land them by glider close to the hotel and then storm the building, freeing Mussolini.

A battalion of paratroopers were to lead the assault, with a road party seizing the cable car station at the foot of the mountain, while a 90-strong group of Student's men would land in a dozen gliders on a meadow outside the hotel. Skorzeny managed to persuade Student to let him and 18 of his SS men go along on the operation, which was actually under the command of a paratroop officer.

The assault force took off from a German-controlled airfield near Rome early in the afternoon of 12 September. Bad weather meant that the senior paratroop officer's glider got lost, leaving Skorzeny's glider as the first one to reach the objective. In a matter of minutes, the SS officer's glider had crash-landed and he raced into the hotel with a handful of men. Bursting into the hotel reception, Skorzeny kicked an Italian radio operator to the floor and smashed his apparatus. Then more Italians were brushed aside and Mussolini was secured. In the

Skorzeny at the entrance to Budapest Castle after securing both the Hungarian Government and the city in the almost bloodless coup of 16 October 1944. Budapest's mayor – who is clearly present to receive orders – is in the background.

commotion, Skorzeny captured the Italian commander and bullied him into ordering his men to surrender. It was all over. There was some fighting at the cable car station at the foot of the mountain, but the rescue operation had so far been an amazing success.

A Fieseler Storch light observation plane was now called up to evacuate Mussolini to Rome, where he would then be whisked away to Germany to be reunited with Hitler. The small aircraft only just managed to set down safely on the 250m- (273yd-) long meadow and, as it turned around to prepare to take off, Skorzeny decided to join the "Duce" for the flight to Rome. At first the pilot refused, but Skorzeny bullied him into letting him on board the two-seat plane, wedged in behind Mussolini.

Amazingly, the Storch made it into the air after its short take-off run. The relieved pilot then turned for Rome and Mussolini was safely delivered into the hands of the Luftwaffe for the flight to Munich. Within hours Nazi radio was broadcasting the news with glee. Hitler heaped praised on Skorzeny and his SS men. The Austrian was awarded the Knight's Cross and was firmly established as someone who could deliver good news to the Führer. Student and his paratroopers were ignored in the rush to praise the SS special forces. This was no accident. Hitler wanted to glorify his elite SS men at the expense of the Luftwaffe paratroopers.

The leader of the Yugoslav communist partisan movement, Josip Broz – Marshal Tito – had long been a thorn in the side of German occupation forces in the Balkans. In three years of war, Tito had managed to raise a large partisan force in the mountainous interior of Yugoslavia, tying down 700,000 German troops by early 1944.

Ironically, given the rivalry between the Abwehr and the SS, Admiral Canaris discovered the location of Tito's mountain headquarters in the town of Drvar, in what is now western Bosnia. German Army commanders in the Balkans organized a corps-sized operation to surround and then destroy the partisan base. As the ground operation got under way, the 500th SS Parachute Battalion was to land by glider around Tito's headquarters, storm its caves and capture the partisan leader, as well the British, Russian and American advisors working with him.

Operation Knight's Move was compromised from the start by partisan agents who spotted the movement of the ground troops towards Drvar, so when the first gliders started landing on 24 May 1944 they were met by fully alert defenders. The first wave of SS men was massacred by Yugoslav fire, allowing Tito to escape down a rope ladder. He was soon on his personal train and heading for safety. More paratroopers landed and soon they were fighting hand-to-hand with the partisans. By the time the ground column relieved the SS detachment, it was all but wiped out. More than 250 Germans were killed and 880 wounded in the operation. Not surprisingly, this was one mission the publicity conscious Skorzeny was not keen to be associated with.

His jagdverbande were busy building up their operations on the Eastern Front during this period, as it became clear that a major Russian offensive was building. When the German Army Group Centre was smashed in July 1944, huge numbers of Germans were trapped behind Soviet lines in so-called "roving pockets". Radio contact was established with several of these groups of desperate men. Jagdverbande East was ordered to organize detachments to parachute in to establish communications with them. KG 200 flew deep behind Soviet lines and dropped the SS teams on their dangerous missions. All except one group were quickly cornered by the Red Army and wiped out. The surviving group linked up with a large "roving pocket" and set up an air bridge to bring in supplies. In spite of remaining at large for several months, eventually they too succumbed.

After the Budapest coup, Skorzeny's men remained at post to secure the city. This is one of the four Tiger IIs of the 503rd Heavy Tank Battalion which took part. Though these are army vehicles, also present here are members of Skorzeny's 500th SS Parachute Battalion.

When the Soviets smashed the German forces in Romania in August 1944, Skorzeny's Jagdverbande Southeast was caught in the rout and destroyed. As Soviet troops surged through the Balkans, clearing Romania and Bulgaria of Axis forces, Hitler was increasingly worried that Hungary was about to switch sides. This was just a situation that required the attention of Skorzeny's talents.

The Führer's suspicions proved correct, as the Hungarian leader Admiral Horthy had long been in negotiations with the Allies to desert the Axis. Skorzeny led an intelligence-gathering mission to the Hungarian capital Budapest, to find out exactly what was going on. Working largely in civilian clothes, he was able to infiltrate the heart of Horthy's regime.

Rival contingents of German and Hungarian troops were watching each other in Budapest with suspicion, as Soviet troops closed on the country's borders. With the German garrison of Budapest called away to counter the Soviet move in October, this was supposed to be the moment Horthy would make his move. Skorzeny struck first. A team of SD men in civilian clothes lured Horthy's son into a trap. Soon he was on his way to a concentration camp in Germany, as a way to ensure his father's loyalty.

THE SS IN BUDAPEST

SS troops were massed around Budapest ready to strike against Horthy's regime, with the ruthless SS general Erich von dem Bach-Zelewski put in charge of the coup. He had just overseen the operation to crush the Polish revolt in Warsaw, and was keen to teach the treacherous Hungarians a lesson by blasting to rubble Budapest's Burgberg Citadel with the giant railway-mounted 650mm Karl mortar.

Fortunately, Skorzeny was able to convince Bach-Zelewski that more subtle methods could do the trick. On 15 October, Horthy made a radio announcement of his intention to negotiate an armistice with the Soviets to save Hungary from becoming a battleground. Later that evening, Operation Panzerfaust was set in motion.

As the Waffen-SS *Maria Theresia* Cavalry Division moved to set up a cordon around the Burgberg to trap Horthy and his government, Skorzeny organized his assault column. He was able to muster several hundred men of the 500th SS Parachute Battalion, Jagdverbande Centre and four Tiger II tanks of the 503rd Heavy Panzer Battalion for his assault group. A detachment of Goliath robot demolition tanks was to tag along behind his column, ready to blast a path through any roadblocks.

At 06:00 hours on 16 October, Skorzeny led his column up the winding road towards the citadel. He was in the cab of the lead truck with two trusted comrades, with the Tigers close behind. In the winter gloom, the first Hungarian checkpoints waved the column of German trucks and tanks past. Skorzeny coolly returned the sentry's salutes. When the SS men ran into a roadblock made of rubble at the gates to the Burgberg, Skorzeny pulled his truck to one side and let the Tigers roll forward. The barricade collapsed under the weight of a 71-tonne (70-ton) tank, and as it emerged into the citadel courtyard the panzer commander swung his 88mm cannon towards a battery of anti-tank guns guarding the seat of the Hungarian government. SS men stormed past the tank, pushing the surprised defenders to the ground and disarming them.

Meanwhile, Skorzeny put his pistol to the head of a Hungarian officer and demanded to be taken to the commandant of the citadel. A further dose of Skorzeny bluster did the trick and the Hungarian officer surrendered his men, in the interests of avoiding bloodshed. Several Hungarians failed to get the order to surrender and started firing at the SS men. Two panzerfaust shells soon silenced the unlucky Hungarians. Unfortunately for Skorzeny, he not did have the honour of seizing Horthy. The Hungarian leader's apartment was empty. He had already left the building to seek the protection of a senior SS officer, who had been related to the former German Kaiser, thinking this would guarantee him better treatment than if he surrendered to an Austrian Nazi thug like Skorzeny.

THE END OF HORTHY'S REGIME

The rest of Skorzeny's men were now moving to seize the other Hungarian ministries around the city, and a brisk firefight broke out at the Ministry of War. Four Germans were killed in the action and three Hungarians died fighting off the SS attack before they received the surrender order.

With the seat of government secure and Horthy in German custody, SS troops moved to occupy the remainder of the city. A puppet regime was installed. Skorzeny, however, had the privilege of escorting Horthy to his new home in a Bavarian castle.

The defeat of German armies in Normandy and the Allied advance to the borders of the Reich in the autumn of 1944 forced Hitler to consider desperate measures to stave off defeat. He was convinced that if the Allies could be dealt a heavy blow in the West this would impel the British and Americans out of the war, giving his forces a free hand to push the Russians back from the Reich's eastern borders. It was complete fantasy, but the Führer was determined to rebuild his armies in time to attack in late November 1944. Obsessed by security, Hitler imposed unprecedented measures to ensure his forces would have the element of surprise when they attacked. Only a handful of trusted senior officers were let in on the secret. One of these was Skorzeny, who was told before most of the army generals who would lead the attacking troops into the Ardennes.

Operation Watch on the Rhine was to involve a large contingent of Skorzeny's special forces to penetrate behind American lines to seize key bridges ahead of the panzer columns. They would also sabotage fuel dumps and sow confusion among the American forces. Many of

Skorzeny in tropical uniform at the time of Operation Knight's Move, the glider-borne attack on General Tito's headquarters, May 1944.

A Tiger II moves past lines of American prisoners in the first successful days of the German offensive in the Ardennes, December 1944. While US Army infantry were facing Tiger IIs from the front, behind their lines Skorzeny's special forces were spreading panic.

these men were to be English speakers, to allow them to impersonate American soldiers. Skorzeny was tasked with forming special units to undertake this mission.

He began trawling through the Wehrmacht for soldiers who had lived in the United States, and ordered the collection of as many captured US Army vehicles, tanks, weapons and uniforms as possible to outfit his new command. A bureaucratic mistake meant a notice requesting volunteers was distributed to every division in the Wehrmacht, infuriating Skorzeny, who was afraid it would find its way into the hands of Allied intelligence. His fears were justified. In early December, the US Army issued an alert that a German offensive, involving the use of special forces led by Skorzeny, could be expected soon.

Skorzeny's efforts to form a "ghost" US Army unit were far from successful. Only 2 Sherman tanks, 50 jeeps and 70 trucks were delivered to Skorzeny, while the number of English speakers left a lot to desired. Of the 200 men classed as "English" speakers, only 10 could pass as real GIs.

A major change of plan was called for. German Panther tanks and halftracks were converted into "mock" American vehicles, so they could pass as a US Army unit and dodge through the holes in the frontlines during the early days of the offensive. Skorzeny's 150th Panzer Brigade was filled out with survivors of his jagdverbande and the 600th

Two members of Skorzeny's "ghost" US Army unit under arrest in Belgium. Organized in nine four-man teams, these infiltrators in American uniforms did enormous harm behind the lines.

SS Parachute Battalion (formerly the 500th Battalion). German Army tank crews, panzergrenadiers, anti-tank gunners, radio operators and engineers boosted the strength of Skorzeny's force to some 2500 men. Two battalions of Luftwaffe paratroopers were nominally under his command, but they operated independently of the SS major.

His force was split into a number of distinct elements. Sabotage teams were to destroy key bridges and fuel dumps to prevent the Americans counterattacking. Reconnaissance units were to push deep into US territory to capture bridges along the strategic River Meuse and spread confusion by issuing false orders or switching road signs. It was the task of two panzer battlegroups to exploit breaches in the American lines, to allow the teams dressed in US uniforms to be infiltrated safely.

When the German offensive got under way on 16 December things did not go according to plan. Skorzeny's panzers got stuck in a traffic jam of supply trucks and missed joining the first attack. Nine of his four-man undercover teams did manage to infiltrate successfully behind enemy lines, though, and one even reached the Meuse.

After being escorted into no-man's-land by panzer patrols, Skorzeny's teams raced behind American lines in jeeps. They radioed reports of American movements, cut wires on bridge demolitions and chopped down road signs.

The effect on the Americans was out of all proportion to the numbers of men involved. Once the first team was captured after failing to give the right password at a checkpoint, news of the undercover squads spread like wildfire. American troops became paranoid about German saboteurs. Passwords were not enough, GIs had to know the latest details of baseball teams to pass muster. When a captured Skorzeny commando admitted to wanting to assassinate General Dwight D. Eisenhower, the supreme Allied commander, his headquarters outside Paris was turned into a fortress.

Most of Skorzeny's teams infiltrated American lines in the opening days of the offensive, but they continued to pass back and forth behind US lines for several days. By the end of the German offensive in late December, the Americans claimed to have captured 18 of Skorzeny's men while several others were killed in firefights. All the captured men were executed for wearing American uniforms. They tried to claim they had not been "fighting" in the US uniforms and so were not "breaking" the rules of war. It did them no good. The stories about the attempt to kill Eisenhower especially enraged senior US officers.

The armoured elements of the 150th Panzer Brigade were eventually committed to action by Skorzeny around the town of Malmédy. Their rag-tag collection of captured US and converted German vehicles failed to convince the GIs holding the lines outside the town that they were an American column. Several of the panzers were knocked out, and the force was hammered by artillery fire as it stalled on the outskirts of the town. Skorzeny himself was injured in this battle. His men then found themselves locked into bitter defensive fighting until the end of the month. More than 200 were killed in two weeks of fighting

Skorzeny was then ordered to pull his unit out of the line, to allow it to be disbanded. The survivors were then posted back to

One of Skorzeny's infiltrators, Guenter Billing, faces a US Army firing squad two weeks into the Ardennes Offensive. Although these men claimed that they were combat soldiers and not spies, American military justice decided otherwise.

their old units. Returning to Germany himself, Skorzeny had just mustered together the remnants of his jagdverbande when a Soviet offensive smashed open the Eastern Front in Poland. Within weeks the Red Army was on the River Oder and every unit in the Wehrmacht, including Skorzeny's command, was dispatched to defend the Reich's eastern border. Once at the front, Skorzeny's unit was ordered to hold the Schwedt bridgehead in an infantry role. It held, until being overrun by the Soviet offensive against Berlin, which rolled forward in April. The SS Parachute Battalion was also sent into this maelstrom and shared a similar fate.

Their leader escaped death on the Eastern Front and was captured by the Americans on 15 May. But his daredevil exploits were far from over. The Americans tried to convict him as a war criminal for sending his men into action wearing US uniforms. After a British officer testified on his behalf about Allied agents and commandos fighting in German uniforms, Skorzeny was acquitted.

The end of Guenter Billing and Skorzeny's plans to undermine the US Army's will to fight. Outraged at Skorzeny's tactics, the Americans attempted to convict him of war crimes in 1945.

He turned the tables on his captors by escaping from a prison camp in 1947 and making his way to Juan Peron's Argentina. He then helped other Nazis escape from Europe as part of the infamous ODESSA network. Not content to lay low like other Nazis, Skorzeny penned his memoirs (at least four times) and freely granted scores of interviews, glorifying his exploits as Hitler's top commando. True to form, he vastly inflated his role in the war and the significance of his exploits. He remained a larger-than-life character right up until his death in Madrid in 1975.

CHAPTER 11

V Weapons –
The Rocket Elite

The V Weapons developed by Nazi scientists during the latter stages

of World War II could have changed the course of the war.

Unmanned and possessing good range, especially the V-2, they could

strike targets anywhere in Great Britain and in Allied-occupied terri-

tory on the continent. They were real terror weapons, and during

their brief careers they spread death and demoralization among

both Allied civilians and military personnel alike.

W orld War II was not just fought by armies, navies and air forces. Whole societies were mobilized to fight in what became known as a "total war". It was no longer enough for a country to have an army packed with brave and determined soldiers – they had to be equipped with more advanced tanks, aircraft, guns, submarines and other weapons than their enemies. Technological superiority brought victory in battle. Eventually Hitler mobilized German society for total war, and his scientists and engineers became an integral part of the Third Reich's war machine. Superior German science would provide its armies with the means to defeat her enemies.

In the Führer's quest for "wonder" weapons to win the war at a stroke, the scientific, industrial and military elite of Germany became merged together in a common endeavour. Ultimately, the scientists and technicians who built and operated Hitler's Vergeltungswaffen, or Reprisal Weapons, which are known to the world as the V Weapons, were all drafted into the military, as a prelude to being brought under

The A-4 (V-2) was the world's first ballistic missile – a strategic weapon against which there was no defence. Thankfully for the Allies, its development would be plagued throughout the war by political in-fighting among the Nazi hierarchy.

Wernher von Braun, technical head of the V-2 project (centre with broken arm in plaster cast), in US Army custody, April 1945. Having escaped from the SS on 6 April, von Braun led his team into the Bavarian alps in the hope of contacting forward units of the US Army.

the control of the SS. They were a new type of warrior, and in the final year of World War II they unleashed death and destruction on targets in Great Britain and western Europe. The British regarded the V Weapon personnel as a deadly foe, and a major objective of the RAF bombing raid on the V Weapon test centre at Peenemünde in August 1943 was to kill as many of them as possible.

ROCKET ELITE

In the 1920s, a group of young German scientists formed a society to develop rockets for interplanetary travel. They experimented with rockets to fire projectiles high into the atmosphere. These burned highly combustible fuel to create thrust. One of the most talented and dynamic of these early rocket enthusiasts was a 19-year-old student named Wernher von Braun. He would later become famous as the man who designed the US Apollo rockets that took men to the Moon in 1969.

Soon the German Army began to take an interest in the work of the rocket scientists and, as early as 1929, conducted experiments with the devices at the Kummersdorf proving ground. A young army captain with a degree in mechanical engineering, Walter Dornberger, supervised these first rocket trials. He would later rise to be Hitler's rocket chief and the nearest equivalent Germany had to Brigadier-General Leslie Grove, who headed the Manhattan Project which developed the atomic bomb for the United States.

By the early 1930s, von Braun and many of his colleagues were working for Dornberger as part of the army's experimental rocket programme. The aim of the programme was to find out if rockets had military applications and could be turned into effective weapons. The initial ideas were modest and had limited tactical applications. In 1934,

Above: The Peenemünde missile complex was hit by a raid of 600 RAF bombers on 17 August 1943, completely devastating the production and assembly works, as well as workers' quarters. It had taken Allied Intelligence 11 months to identify the site after the launch of the first A-4 prototype in October 1942.

Left: Once built, the V-2s left the factory by train for distribution to their launch teams; ideally to be launched within three days.

the first Germany military rocket, the A-2, was test fired and achieved a range of some two kilometres (6500ft). Two years later, work had progressed so far that the Army High Command literally gave Dornberger and von Braun a blank cheque to develop long-range weapons. They began planning the building of a firing range where the weapons could be tested in secret, and soon work started to construct the Peenemünde research centre on the Baltic coast. The Luftwaffe also began to build a test facility nearby, but its activities were largely separate from those under the control of the Army Weapons Department. Eventually more than 3000 people would be working at the site, which boasted laboratories, assembly plants, test ranges, an air-field and its own power station. At today's prices, building the site cost nearly $2 billion US. It was up and running by 1940, in time for the rocket programme to move into high gear.

The defeat of the Luftwaffe bombing offensive against Britain during the summer of 1940 gave the rocket programme its first big boost, as Hitler looked for a way to strike at his enemy across the English Channel. Work on a rocket, then designated the A-4, was accelerated and by 1942 the first test firing was conducted. After two failures, the first successful A-4 launch was conducted on 3 October 1942. Dornberger, now promoted colonel, made the launch countdown. The rocket broke the sound barrier, entered space and re-entered the atmosphere. During a flight that lasted little over a minute, the rocket flew more than 190km (117 miles) out into the Baltic Sea, impacting only 4km (2.5 miles) from its intended target.

THE V-2

When Hitler heard the news of the successful trial he was excited, and within months had ordered his new armaments minister, Albert Speer, to put the A-4 into production. Dubbed the Vergeltungswaffe 2, or V-2, it was to be the first ballistic missile to be used in combat. The production versions were some 14m (49ft) high, 1.65m (6ft) in diameter and weighed more than 12,000kg (26,400lb). They could carry a 1000kg (2200lb) explosive warhead up to 340km (210 miles), thanks to a rocket motor powered by liquid oxygen and alcohol.

Dornberger and his army colleagues insisted, over the wishes of the scientists, that the weapon be made mobile. A fixed base, no matter

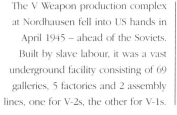

The V Weapon production complex at Nordhausen fell into US hands in April 1945 – ahead of the Soviets. Built by slave labour, it was a vast underground facility consisting of 69 galleries, 5 factories and 2 assembly lines, one for V-2s, the other for V-1s.

how well protected by concrete, would be far too vulnerable to Allied bombers. The V-2s were to be launched from large trailer-mounted launchers that could be assembled in a few hours.

A huge production network was established to start mass producing the weapons, with final assembly to take place in vast purpose-built halls in Peenemünde, Austria and northern Germany. At peak rate, it was planned to build 950 rockets a month to blast Great Britain into submission. Dornberger was promoted to major-general to oversee the expanded Peenemünde operations, and later rose to the rank of lieutenant-general. By now von Braun and his fellow scientists at the Baltic test centre had been drafted into the army as part of the mysteriously titled "Experimental Detachment North". Every one of these "scientist soldiers" had a military rank but they still called each other by their first names. By the summer of 1943, Training and Experimental Battery 444 was set up to train the soldiers who would eventually fire the weapons. Some 12,000 people were now working at the centre.

All through 1943 the test programme to finalize the V-2 design gathered pace and work began on longer-range versions. This all came to an abrupt halt when RAF Bomber Command raided Peenemünde on the night of 17/18 August. The 227 bombers largely missed the vital A-4 test facilities, instead putting most of their bombs on a prison camp for the slave labour used in the factories at the centre, killing more than 700 unfortunate prisoners.

The Germans decided to close down Peenemünde, not because of the damage caused but because they realized that the above-ground

Unlike the V-2 missile, the V-1 was a pilotless aircraft powered by a pulse jet. The prototype first flew from Peenemünde on 24 December 1942 and went into action on 13 June 1944, when 10 were launched against southern England.

facilities at the site were too vulnerable. Test ranges were opened deep in Poland and an underground factory was to be built under a mountain at Nordhausen in central Germany. Peenemünde, however, remained a key administrative centre for the V-2 programme. The decline of Germany's fortunes on the battlefields of Europe made Hitler more desperate to get the V-2s into action, and the production target was increased to 2000 a month. Delays and technical problems meant production lagged far behind schedule. In January 1944 only 140 V-2s were completed. This rose to a peak of 600 in August of that a year, and by the end of the war some 6000 had been built.

In spite of earlier predictions about the risk of bomber attacks on fixed launch sites, two huge concrete launch bunkers were built in France in early 1944. True to form the RAF and United States Army Air Force (USAAF) destroyed them before they could be completed.

Dornberger and von Braun had to fall back on their mobile launchers, and preparations gathered pace during the summer of 1944 for the rocket offensive to get under way. Two launch contingents were formed, one based on Battery 444 and another designated Group North. Scientists and other Peenemünde experts joined these units, which moved to secret launch sites around the Dutch capital, The Hague, because Allied armies had driven the Germans back from their original launch sites in France and Belgium. The first ever combat launch of a V-2 was carried out by Battery 444 on the morning of 8 September 1944. The target was Paris. Later that day Group North fired another V-2 at London.

Over the next eight months more than 2500 V-2s were launched against southeast England, the Belgian port of Antwerp and Paris. Antwerp was the main target, with 1712 rockets being fired at the port, which was a key supply base for Allied

The warhead of the V-1 consisted of 841kg (1870lb) of high-explosive held directly behind the compass and giros in the nose. The fuel tanks were between the wings, behind which were two tanks of compressed air which powered the control surfaces located in the tail.

forces on the continent. London was on the receiving end of 517 V-2s. There was no defence against the supersonic rockets.

When the Dutch Resistance began radioing the locations of the launch sites around The Hague, Allied bombers were sent into action. The time it took to transmit the information to the Allies meant the launch teams were long gone before the bombers arrived. No sites were hit by the bombers, and the Allies had to resort to bombing German supply lines to prevent fuel and new rockets reaching the launch units.

The launch units, however, suffered casualties in the course of their work, mainly when rockets failed immediately after launch and fell back to earth. Some 20 percent of rockets failed and scores of them fell back into The Hague, killing and injuring Dutch civilians. As the V-2 campaign gathered momentum the crews gained experience, allowing them to set up their launch platforms in a matter of minutes and then quickly evacuate before Allied bombers could arrive.

Although the pulse jet could attain speeds of 640kph (400mph), the V-1 – weighing 2180kg (4796lb) – needed extra thrust at take-off. This was supplied by a piston-like catapult on the launch ramp powered by a hydrogen-peroxide propellant.

Through the winter of 1944 and into 1945, the V-2 crews kept up their deadly barrage, and only the advance of Allied troops into Germany forced the launch batteries to pull out of Holland. The last V-2 was fired on 27 March 1945, against London, landing in Whitechapel and killing 134 people. Two days later the V-2 units retreated from The Hague.

THE V-1

Separate from Dornberger and von Braun's efforts to built ballistic rockets, the Luftwaffe High Command was developing its own long-range missile. It had seen how much money and prestige the army had gained from the Peenemünde rocket programmes and wanted a percentage of these resources. In the late 1930s, the Luftwaffe contracted the Fieseler company, which designed the famous Storch light aircraft, to build a jet-powered subsonic, winged missile. The Fi 103 first flew in December 1941 from a ramp at the Luftwaffe's

section of the Peenemünde range. Compared to the A-4/V-2 the Fi 103, or V-1 as it was soon designated, was cheap and easy to produce and operate. It was launched from simple concrete and steel rails and could fly to ranges of between 250km and 320km (155 miles to 198 miles). This weapon was the forerunner of the modern-day cruise missiles, such as the US Tomahawk.

Mass production was ordered by Hitler in 1942, as a back-up in case the V-2 project did not come to fruition. It was intended that 2000 a month would be rolling off Fieseler's production line. The flak or anti-aircraft branch of the Luftwaffe was given responsibility for the V-1 programme. In August 1943, Flak Regiment 155 (W) was formed under the command of Colonel Max Washtel to establish a network of launch sites along the north coast of France and Belgium to begin the bombardment of England.

V-1 LAUNCH SITES

As with the V-1 programme, initial efforts concentrated on building fixed launch sites. Work began in the autumn of 1943 to build 88 of them, but British intelligence soon learned the purpose of the so-called "ski sites". Allied bombers then systematically attacked the sites during December and into 1944. Flak Regiment 155 had more than 5700 men available in March 1944 as preparations began to get the V-1 offensive back on track. Colonel Washtel and his boss, Lieutenant-General Walter von Axhelm, devised new tactics to defeat the Allied bombing threat.

The new launch sites were small and dispersed around the countryside, with camouflage replacing concrete as the main means of protection. Cheap prefabricated launch rails were designed. The firing batteries moved constantly between launch sites to avoid detection by Allied aircraft. Dummy sites further confused Allied intelligence.

In the run-up to the D-Day landings in June 1944, Allied bombers and resistance saboteurs devastated the French rail network, playing havoc with the final preparations to launch the first V-1s against England. It had been intended to launch a mass salvo from 54 sites. In the end, only seven sites could be made ready for operations on the night of 12 June and they fired 10 V-1s. Three days later the pace of firing increased when 55 sites were up and running, launching 244 V-1s.

By the end of June the Germans were launching 120–190 V-1s a day, and 2000 weapons had been fired at England, the majority landing around London. The V-1s suffered from one major disadvantage, once launched they had to fly on a constant course and altitude at 640kph (400 mph). This made it relatively easy for fighters to intercept and shoot them down, or deflect them off course by "tipping" the wings. Anti-aircraft batteries and barrage balloons could also be placed along likely approach routes to obvious targets.

After the initial surprise of the first V-1s, soon dubbed "Doodlebugs", "Buzz Bombs" or "Flying Bombs", the British quickly built up their

Like the V-2, the V-1 was a terror weapon – landing indiscriminately on civilian targets, as shown here. Some warning was given during the first V-1 attacks because the pulse jet would cut out in the final dive. This, however, was a design fault and was soon rectified.

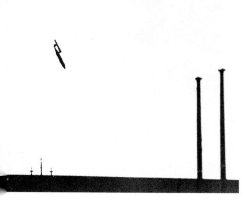

defences and began to intercept a significant number of the German weapons. The Allied advances across France in the summer of 1944 further hampered the activities of Regiment 155 so, by the end of August, the first phase of the V-1 offensive was over after the launching of 8554 of the weapons.

With its launch sites gone, the Luftwaffe turned to using converted Heinkel He 111 bombers to launch a V-1 slung under the fuselage. Kampfgruppe 53 was specially trained to fly these missions, beginning in September 1944. Over the next four months, just under 900 V-1s were launched against Great Britain by the special Heinkel unit.

Regiment 155 was in the process of pulling back into German and Holland and reorganizing itself to renew operations. A new version of the V-1, with wooden wings and enough range to hit London from inside Holland, was also being developed. During the winter months of 1944, the regiment concentrated on bombarding Antwerp, Brussels and Liège with some 8000 V-1s. Once the extended-range version was available they began to be fired against England. Some 275 were fired before V Weapon operations were suspended on 30 March 1944. By the end of the war 30,000 V-1s had been built and 18,000 had been

launched against targets in Great Britain and western Europe.

Even before the first V-1s and V-2s were fired in anger, their potential as possible war-winning weapons was recognized by Heinrich Himmler, head of the SS. He was determined that the SS would control and take the glory for these weapons. In February 1944, Himmler began to pressure von Braun to transfer from the army to the SS. When persuasion failed, he had him and several other key scientists working at Peenemünde arrested on the charge that they were wasting valuable resources on peaceful space exploration rather than creating weapons of war. Dornberger, who was now the army's commissioner for special duties in charge of the development, training and operations of V-2 units, was able to secure the scientists' release after several days, claiming the rocket programme was falling behind without their expertise.

In the wake of the July 1944 bomb plot to kill Hitler, the SS moved fast to secure control of the V Weapons. SS Lieutenant-General Hans Kammler, head of the SS construction office, was appointed to lead the SS V

By January 1945, as battle fronts collapsed, even mobile launch units were not able to fire V-2s at a high enough rate. Experiments were made to transport, fuel and launch the missiles direct from specially converted trains.

Weapon division, with Dornberger reduced to the status of his deputy. In January 1945, Kammler had managed to expand his empire to include full control of the Luftwaffe's V-1 programme.

Kammler played a key role in controlling the V-2 operations in Holland, with SS units providing security for the launch sites around The Hague. They forcibly evicted hundreds of residents from around the launch sites to prevent them being observed. When the rocket units were forced out of Holland in April 1945, he regrouped the men around the Nordhausen factory to stage a last stand as infantry.

Hitler's interest in wonder weapons was not just restricted to rockets and missiles. He got very excited when the Rochling Iron and Steel company proposed building a long-range gun that could bombard London from France and demanded that work on the weapon start immediately. He saw this weapon as his London Gun, a worthy successor to the Paris Gun that the Kaiser's army had used to bombard the French capital in World War I. The aim was to build a battery of 50 weapons that could fire 600 140kg (308lb) shells at London every day.

Dubbed the High Pressure Pump or HDP Gun, the weapon was built around a 130m- (142yd-) long smoothbore barrel that had propellant charges positioned along its length. As the shell progressed up the barrel the extra charges kicked in, rapidly building up the velocity to the speed required to carry the projectile to its target. To support the barrel, it had been constructed on the side of a hill. This was the weapon that would inspire the Canadian scientist Gerald Bull to build the Super Gun for Iraqi dictator Saddam Hussein in the 1980s.

While tests of the new weapon, now dubbed the V-3, got under way in Poland during late 1943 and into 1944, work began on the first gun emplacement in the Pas-de-Calais. RAF bombers soon destroyed the site and the "London Gun" never fired a shot across the Channel. The army formed Artillery Battalion 705 to operate the new weapon, which by late 1944 was to be emplaced in western German to bombard France, Belgium and Luxembourg.

RIVAL SS PROGRAMMES

The SS grab for the V Weapon programme brought the V-3 under Kammler's control late in 1944, and he ordered work to be accelerated to enable the weapon to support the German offensive in the Ardennes in December 1944. The first shells were fired in anger on 30 December. Eventually, a second weapon was brought into action and they both continued firing regularly through to the middle of February when US Army troops overran the positions. Some 163 shells were fired in total, to little effect. The Germans managed to pull back the weapons themselves, but no further use could be found for them.

Even before the SS gained official control of the V Weapons, it was keen to develop rival long-range weapons to those being built by the German Army and Luftwaffe. After the Rheinmetall-Borsig company had its design for a solid-fuel, long-range rocket rejected by Dornberger, they turned to the field artillery and then the SS to support their project. Solid fuel offered the possibility of reducing the size of the rockets and improving safety, the liquid fuel of the V-2 being notoriously unreliable and highly dangerous for its launch crews.

The arrow-like Rh-Z-61, or Rheinbote, was eventually able to fly 194km (120 miles) and was the first multi-stage rocket ever to be used in combat.

With the help of Rheinmetall-Borsig technicians, Artillery Battery 709 was up and running by 24 December 1944, and fired a salvo of 24 Rheinbotes, now designated the V-4, against Antwerp. Even the normally enthusiastic Kammler was not convinced about the effectiveness of the weapons, which seemed to be very inaccurate, and he ordered the termination of firings after another 20 rockets had been launched at the Belgian port.

THE LEGACY

The impact of the V Weapon programme on the outcome of the war was limited. Of the 10,000 or so V-1s launched at England, more than 3000 misfired or crashed en route and 4000 were intercepted by British defences. Out of the remaining weapons, only 2500 reached their intended target, London, and none hit their aim point, Tower Bridge. More than 6000 people were killed, 40,000 injured and 20,000 houses destroyed in the V-1 offensive against Britain. A further 3000 people were killed and 7000 injured in V-2 strikes on London. This compared to 40,000 killed and 46,000 injured during the day and night bombing of Great Britain in 1940–41. In spite of the inability of the defences to provide protection from the V-2, British morale did not crack. The war was clearly being won on the ground in Europe and the British public were willing to hang on until the Allied armies achieved victory. The level of damage was not unbearable, while V Weapon attacks on Antwerp and other Allied supply bases on the continent were never accurate enough or sustained enough to prevent the build-up of resources needed by the massive armies poised to invade Germany.

The huge human, material and technological resources thrown into the V Weapon programme were in vain. The Führer's dream of using Germany's scientific superiority to defeat his enemies at a stroke proved a delusion. It would be Germany's enemies who eventually realized this dream.

Hitler's V Weapon programme saw the first use of ballistic missiles, cruise missiles and other exotic weapons in combat. The men who built and used these weapons were a new type of warrior. Scientists, engineers and military men worked hand-in-glove to perfect and employ revolutionary new weapons of war. They were the forebears of the men who built the weapons of mass destruction that dominated the Cold War. Von Braun and his associates at Peenemünde were already thinking about their postwar futures in February 1944, when they began to evacuate their research centre for a sector of Germany that was likely to fall under American, rather than Soviet, control. Within months of Germany's surrender, von Braun and almost 500 German rocket scientists were on their way to the United States to help build the first US rockets that eventually allowed men to travel to the Moon. Their usefulness to the US Government meant they escaped prosecution for war crimes.

Left: After the US Army had captured the Nordhausen complex, plans were made to ship as much as was moveable west in the face of the Soviet advance. By 22 May 1945, 12 tonnes (11 tons) of documents and 300 rail wagons full of V-2 parts were on their way to Antwerp.

Right: The Rheinbote was a surface-to-surface missile developed for the German Army in late 1944. It was a four-stage missile of 1.7 tonnes (1.6 tons) running on solid propellant, but carried a warhead of only 40kg (20lb). Just 220 were produced.

CHAPTER 12

JV 44 – The Galland Circus

Adolf Galland was Germany's top fighter ace, and as the Third Reich began to fragment he was given command of a squadron of fighter aces and new jet fighter aircraft. This new unit was never going to change the course of the war, but it left a legacy of courage and glory that typified its commander. The unit became the "Galland Circus", operated according to its own code of honour, and largely ignored the dictates of senior Nazi officials.

Adolf Galland was one of the most famous Bf 109 aces of World War II, being credited with 103 confirmed victories by 1941. Promoted to command the Luftwaffe's fighter branch, he became a vociferous promoter of the Me 262 fighter jet.

A s the Third Reich entered its death throes, the Luftwaffe formed an elite fighter unit to fly the world's first operational jet fighter aircraft – the Messerschmitt Me 262. Commanded by a lieutenant-general and bringing together the Luftwaffe's top fighter aces, Jagdverbande 44, or JV 44, symbolized on the one hand the bankruptcy of Hitler's military strategy but at the same time showed that the fighting spirit of Germany's elite warriors was not yet broken. Outnumbered and fighting a hopeless cause, the pilots of JV 44 still took to the skies until only a few days before the Third Reich surrendered.

The unit was formed and led by the famous fighter ace Adolf Galland, who by 1945 had notched up 103 confirmed kills in the skies over Spain, Poland, France and Russia. In November 1941, at only 32 years of age, Galland had been promoted to major-general and appointed to lead the Luftwaffe's fighter branch. His reputation was such that, within hours of being put in charge of forming JV 44, he was being bombarded with requests to join his "squadron of experts", which soon became known as the "Galland Circus" in the manner of World War I fighter squadrons.

ME 262

The fighter that gave the Galland Circus its edge in combat over Allied fighters in the skies of Germany was the Messerschmitt Me 262 "Swallow". The sleek, two-engined fighter was the world's first operational jet fighter aircraft. Powered by Junkers Jumo 004 jet engines, the Me 262 could reach speeds in excess of 800kph (500mph) and had a climb rate of more than 1200m (3900ft) a minute. This performance gave its pilots an impressive advantage over Allied aircraft, including the Gloster Meteor jets just entering service with the Royal Air Force (RAF).

The Me 262 was the culmination of years of work to create jet combat aircraft begun by German aviation pioneers in the 1930s. First to begin work was the Heinkel Company, but in 1939 the German Air Ministry issued an order to

The Honour Standard of the Condor Legion presented by a grateful General Franco on the legion's departure from Spain in April 1939. The Spanish Civil War proved an excellent training ground for the Luftwaffe's pilots. Galland flew in the legion's three-squadron fighter group.

Messerschmitt to begin work on another design. The eventual result was the distinctive swept-wing shape that became the Me 262. Work progressed slowly, and the first prototype flew in 1941 with propeller engines because the jets were not ready. The first jet-powered Me 262 flew a few months later, but an engine failure on take-off forced a redesign with the newer and more reliable Jumo 004 engines. Superb performance in test flights resulted in the Luftwaffe selecting the aircraft for production in May 1943, and the rival Heinkel design was cancelled.

At this time Galland began his association with the Me 262 after being given the chance to test fly the aircraft. He immediately recognized the potential of the new aircraft, and recommended it immediately go into production to boost Germany's fighter strength. It was the only German fighter that had the speed and performance to match the British wooden de Havilland Mosquito fighter-bombers that were then ranging freely over Germany. Hitler was given a demonstration of the jet later in 1943 and instantly decided to order it as a bomber. Before production was fully up and running, a raid by the USAAF destroyed the Messerschmitt assembly line at Regensburg, setting back the programme by several months while production was moved deep into Bavaria.

While the performance of the Me 262 was impressive, it was a far from easy aircraft to fly, taxing even the most experienced pilot. Ground handling was difficult and it had a tendency to flip over if the pilot lost control. Even more worrying was its high stall speed – 288kph (180mph) – which, combined with the unreliable Jumo 004 powerplant, meant that an engine failure could result in a catastrophic stall. At high speeds the aircraft was far from stable, which significantly reduced the accuracy of its weapons. It was also took a highly skilled pilot to master the art of engaging targets in the fleeting moments an Allied aircraft was in the jet's sights during a high-speed attack run. The engines themselves had be overhauled after nine hours flight and scrapped after 25 hours. This gives some idea of the enormous technical and logistical challenges required to keep the Me 262s in the air.

Major Galland in the cockpit of his Bf 109E-4 during the Battle of Britain, 1940. Though the battle was a defeat for the Luftwaffe – and Hermann Goering – it brought Galland personal victories and national fame in Germany.

The armament of the basic Me 262 was four 30mm cannons mounted in the nose, with 360 rounds of ammunition available. Two 30mm cannons were carried in the reconnaissance version, which had nose-mounted cameras. As experience was gained with the aircraft, different armament packages were adopted to allow the jet to take on Allied heavy bombers, including a 50mm long-barrelled nose cannon and underwing R4M unguided rockets. These rockets were to be fired in a salvo at an enemy bomber, and the spread of weapons was intended to devastate the aircraft. Work was started on guided rockets, but these were not ready for service before the end of the war. In the ground-attack role, two 250kg (550lb) bombs were carried on racks under the forward fuselage.

By early 1944, production was in high gear and the first of 1000 Me 262s were being delivered to the Luftwaffe. Hitler's insistence on the jets being used as bombers meant that, as Allied aircraft pounded the German Army in Normandy, there were few Me 262 fighters available to resist the onslaught. By early 1945, seven Luftwaffe groups were equipped with the Me 262 in fighter, ground-attack and reconnaissance roles. The rapid advance of Allied and Soviet armies meant the Luftwaffe was forced back to a reduced number of airfields inside the borders of Germany. Every day, thousands of Allied aircraft dropped thousands of tonnes of bombs on Germany and there was little the remnants of the Lutfwaffe could do about it. The mixing of inexperienced pilots, including former bomber pilots, within the Me 262 units meant the senior Luftwaffe fighter officers, such as Galland, thought the jets were not being used as effectively as they thought possible. The lamentable performance of the Luftwaffe in the final months of 1944 drove its top fighter pilots to question the leadership of Goering, and actually call for his dismissal. Galland was the ringleader of this group.

Johannes Steinhoff, fighter ace and one of the senior combat pilots who openly sided with Galland in his row with Goering in early 1945.

It was not really a surprise that Galland was at the centre of this effort to challenge Goering's disastrous policies. He had famously enraged the corpulent Luftwaffe chief at the height of the Battle of Britain in 1940 by telling Goering that he needed a squadron of Spitfires to defeat the Royal Air Force.

Famous for his movie star good looks and cocky fighter pilot swagger, Galland flew 300 missions with the German Condor Legion during the Spanish Civil War, before commanding a squadron of Messerschmitt Bf 109 fighters during the Polish and French campaigns. Promoted to major during the Battle of Britain after pushing his kill tally up to 70 aircraft, he was a lieutenant-colonel by the end of September 1940, coming to the notice of the Luftwaffe High Command and the Führer.

Rather than join the forces massing to invade Russia, Galland's unit remained in France duelling with RAF fighters sent to sweep northern France. His fighters covered the famous "Channel Dash" by two German battleships in February 1942, and he pushed his kill total up to 94 confirmed kills. Compared to his comrades who were fighting in Russia, Galland's kill total was modest, but the vast majority of his aerial victories were against RAF and American pilots in high-performance Spitfires, Hurricanes or Mustangs. The need to counter these top-of-the-range Western machines meant Galland was always looking to develop better tactics and aircraft. Not surprisingly, as a fighter pilot he passionately believed that without air supremacy Germany would lose the war, and often clashed with senior Luftwaffe offices who did not share his ideas. He had little time for strategic bombing theorists.

GALLAND TAKES CHARGE OF THE FIGHTER BRANCH

When Luftwaffe fighter ace Werner Moelders was killed in 1941, the young firebrand Galland was the natural choice to take over his job, leading the Luftwaffe's fighter branch. Although this did not involve the frontline command of fighter units, it did mean Galland was intimately concerned with the design and production of new fighter aircraft for the Luftwaffe, as well as advising on tactics. As the Allied bombing offensive against Germany gathered momentum in 1942 and 1943, Galland pressed repeatedly for priority to be given to building night fighters and jets to counter the thousands of RAF and USAAF heavy bombers raining devastation on Germany's cities. In spite of the impact on industrial production, Hitler and Goering insisted on downgrading fighter production to build bombers or V Weapons. When the American P-51 Mustang fighters started to escort B-17s over Germany in late 1943, there were not enough fighters to take them on. In the first five months of 1944, the Luftwaffe lost more than 1000 experienced fighter pilots in this one-sided duel and there was little prospect of replacing them. By the time the Allies landed in Normandy the fighter arm was crippled. Against Galland's advice the remnants were committed to the defence of Normandy, and were soon decimated. With German

The officer Galland replaced as commander of the fighter branch: General Werner Moelders. Like Galland, Moelders was a Condor Legion veteran and fighter ace. He was the first fighter pilot to be awarded the Knight's Cross and took over the fighter branch in the summer of 1941. He was killed in a plane crash the following November.

The fighter which Adolf Galland believed could turn the tide against the Allied bomber offensive: the Me 262. His optimism was well-founded; the 262's two turbo jets gave the aircraft a climb rate of 1200m (3936ft) per minute and a speed of 868kph (536mph) at 7000m (22,880ft).

war production now being hammered by constant day and night raids, there was little that could be done to rebuild the Luftwaffe. Germany's forward-looking armament's minister, Albert Speer, became a close friend of Galland as he struggled to stave off the total collapse of the Luftwaffe's fighter arm. Galland pleaded for all the available fighters to be massed for "strategic attacks" on Allied bombers. Goering ignored him and wasted the reserves of combat aircraft on the poorly conceived "Bodenplatte" offensive against Allied airfields in western Europe. Galland was scapegoated by Goering and sacked.

This was the background to the so-called "Revolt of the Fighter Pilots" in January 1945. A group of leading Luftwaffe fighter pilots and commanders demanded a meeting with Goering to protest at Galland's sacking and Goering's disastrous policies. One of those present said their demands were simple: "Fatty [Goering] must go." The Luftwaffe chief was outraged at what he called a mutiny and stormed out of the meeting to issue orders for Galland's arrest. Other members of the revolt were relieved of their commands or put on the arrest list. A despairing Galland turned to Speer to help in this desperate situation.

Speer made a personal appeal to Hitler, who still had a soft spot for Galland and several of the other highly decorated members of the mutiny. Goering was instructed to reverse the arrest warrants and give Galland, by then a lieutenant-general, command of a special unit of some 22 Me 262s that was to be a little bigger than a squadron and outside the normal Luftwaffe chain of command. Galland was, in effect, being given the chance to prove his theories about how jet fighters could change the course of the war or die in the process. JV 44 was born.

Goering and his sycophants in the Luftwaffe High Command were far from happy at being overruled by Hitler. They made every effort to sabotage Galland's operation and repeatedly tried to have it disbanded. No mention was allowed to be made of his name in the unit's designation, and he was to receive no help from any Luftwaffe headquarters in organizing the unit. Galland was on his own.

Galland's personal following among Luftwaffe fighter pilots was more than a match for Goering's crude attempts at obstruction. Several senior members of the mutiny, such as Johannes Steinhoff and Gunther Lutzow, were quick to join and, as word spread, top fighter pilots were beating a path to Galland's door. Many of the Luftwaffe's finest knew the end was approaching and wanted to see out the war flying with the best, in the best aircraft. Speer and other friendly industrialists helped to ensure that Galland got the planes, spares and support equipment he needed.

In late February 1945, JV 44 was beginning to take shape at an airfield near Berlin. Its roll of pilots looked like a who's-who of German fighter aces. At least 16 of its pilots wore the Knight's Cross and seven had Oak Leaves. They had a combined kill total of more than 1000 enemy aircraft. Many of them had not flown the Me 262 before, however, and they had to spend a lot of time mastering the temperamental jet.

GALLAND'S NEW TACTICS

To employ the Me 262 to its best advantage, Galland developed new "Schwarme" or swarm tactics that envisaged formations of three jets flying together, termed a Ketten or chain, so their pilots had better observation and could concentrate more firepower against a single target. Once a bomber formation was detected, Galland wanted a full Ketten of three jets to circle around behind the rear of a single bomber and then attack simultaneously. By attacking at maximum speed, the Me 262s would hit their target and accelerate away before the bomber's gunners could find their aim or escorting American fighters would have time to intervene. At least one of the aircraft in the Ketten was to be equipped with R4M rockets to ensure that one way or another the bomber did not survive.

At the end of March 1945, Galland's unit was ready to move south to Munich-Reim air base to begin its brief quest for glory. It flew its first operational patrol on 3 April, without encountering any opposition. A solitary P-38 Lightning reconnaissance aircraft was claimed shot down on 4 April, but at this point there was no sign of any large formations of enemy bombers over southern Germany.

The Galland Circus got the chance to show its mettle two days later, when a formation of more than 1000 Allied bombers and 600 fighters approached southern Germany. Five Me 262s, led by Steinhoff, took off to engage the massive formation. It was a hopeless task, but they still took on the bombers, shooting down one B-17 for the loss of one Me 262. When the surviving jets arrived back at base they found it being strafed by Allied fighters and barely got down safely. This set the scene for the next month, with relentless Allied air attacks on the JV 44 base, forcing the Me 262s to be dispersed into surrounding woods. Focke Wulf Fw 190 fighters were drafted in to protect the jets, which were vulnerable to attack during take-off and landing.

The fame of JV 44 was now spreading throughout the Luftwaffe and senior officers now started to refer to it as "Jagdverbande Galland". It was the ultimate complement to the Luftwaffe's most famous fighter pilot.

Day after day JV 44 pilots got airborne to challenge ever-larger formations of Allied aircraft. On average JV 44 put up two Ketten with six aircraft, whereas the Allies sent over 1000 aircraft daily into the skies over Germany. A USAAF Mustang fell victim to JV 44 on 10 April.

Galland took his share of duty in the air and claimed two kills on 16 April, attacking a formation of B-26 Marauders with R4M rockets. The Americans kept up the pressure on JV 44 when, just after Galland and his men returned to base, 11 Mustangs swooped on Munich-Reim shooting up 25 German aircraft. Amidst this carnage Galland tried to keep his aircraft on alert and scrambled whenever a tempting target came within range. He led his men into action again on the 17th and claimed an American fighter. On one scramble on 18 April, Steinhoff fell

Reichsmarshall Hermann Goering reviews members of the Condor Legion, May 1939. During World War I Goering had been a fighter ace himself and success in Nazi Party politics brought him command of the new Luftwaffe in March 1935. His competence would be questioned by many as the war progressed.

The fighter which in 1940 Adolf Galland dared inform Goering he wanted for his own squadron: the Supermarine Spitfire. This is the cannon-armed Mk V-B variant.

victim to the poor handling characteristics of the Me 262 and was badly burned after his jet overturned on take-off. Three German jets took to the skies again the following day to engage 500 American bombers, and managed to shoot one down.

Better results were achieved on 20 April, when three B-26s were shot down and seven damaged by Galland's aces, using Ketten tactics to good effect, when they surprised a large formation of bombers over Bavaria and escaped before escorting fighters could intervene.

Continuing advances by Allied armies resulted in almost all the remaining Me 262 units gathering their aircraft at Munich-Reim, where they effectively came under Galland's command and brought the number of jets available to more than 40. He could now put more than a dozen aircraft into the air on a daily basis. A further 16 Me 262s, including one of the experimental versions armed with a 50mm cannon, flew south to join Galland on 23 April. Another dozen jets arrived the following day.

This was JV 44's target: massed formations of American B-17 Flying
Fortresses of the US Army Eighth Air
Force, flying "precision" daylight
raids against Germany.

The new arrivals boosted the attack strength of JV 44 and it put up
spirited resistance to raids on 24 April, surprising a US bomber formation in the morning and shooting down three aircraft. More jets went
into action, but American fighters were on hand this time and drove off
the Me 262s. Lutzow's jet was hit and exploded, killing the famous ace
with 108 kills to his name.

Goering now tried to assume control of the German Government
after news emerged that Berlin was surrounded. Hitler was furious and
ordered Goering's arrest. In a bizarre twist, Speer ordered Galland to
arrest his old boss. More interested in defending his country than playing politics, Galland chose to ignore this order.

His pilots did not have long to wait before they were called into
action again. They tried to engage a bomber formation on 25 April and
claimed two American fighters lost in dogfights. During this
engagement, JV 44 tried to employ the Me 262 with the 50mm cannon for the first time. It jammed and no Allied bombers were
blown to pieces by the heavy weapon. Galland himself led his men
into battle the following day against a formation of B-26 Marauders
over Ulm. He quickly shot down two of the bombers with guns,
and two others fell victim to German rockets. The German jets
were then jumped by P-47 Thunderbolt escort fighters. Galland's
cockpit was riddled with bullets and his right leg shattered by

shrapnel. Breaking off the combat, he turned for home and returned to Munich-Reim just as it was being attacked by Allied fighters. He only just managed to get his jet down but it veered off the runway, slithering to a halt as cannon fire burst around his jet. It was the end of his flying career in the Luftwaffe, and Colonel Heinz Bar took command of JV 44.

The following day JV 44 mounted its combat finale, against American fighters attacking from the west and Soviet aircraft from the east. The Me 262s claimed four kills, including two by Bar.

Gallant, his leg in plaster, was back in command of his men, even if he was confined to a hospital bed, when orders were received for his unit to move north to Prague to join the battle against Soviet troops advancing on the Czech capital. Fearing that his men would fall into Soviet captivity if he complied with the orders, Galland refused to obey and instructed Bar to keep JV 44 where it was. After much lobbying by Galland, the orders were changed and the unit began relocating to Salzburg in Austria.

When news came through that Hitler had committed suicide, Galland sent an emissary to negotiate with the Americans. He proposed keeping JV 44 intact for use against the Soviets. They ignored his approach. The Luftwaffe High Command still wanted to move JV 44 to Prague but Bar refused to budge, declaring: "I follow the orders of Lieutenant-General Galland." On 4 May JV 44 surrendered after US Army tanks overran its new base at Salzburg, but not before the pilots had been able to destroy all their aircraft by placing hand grenades in their cockpits.

FINAL RECKONING

Galland later denied that he was some sort of Nazi fanatic who had wanted to prolong the war when he knew Germany's cause was ultimately lost. He claimed his unit was just doing its duty to the end. At the close of hostilities, he had failed to prove that the massed use of Me 262s could defeat the huge Allied bomber formations. The odds were simply overwhelming. He was never able to get more than a dozen jets into air at any one time. When faced by hundreds of bombers and fighters, there was little the "squadron of experts" could do. In its brief 11-week existence, JV 44 only managed to shoot down 24 Allied aircraft for the loss of three Me 262s in air-to-air combat, although dozens of the unit's aircraft were destroyed or damaged in the relentless air raids on its base.

The fate of JV 44 summed up the contribution of elite units to the German war effort. They were a heroic failure. Galland and his men may have gone down fighting, but they were ultimately unable to change the course of the war. Hitler's strategic failures and Allied numerical superiority could not be countered by the bravery of a few men, no matter how well led and equipped.

tage over the other, due mainly to the restraints of the terrain and the difficulties in getting regular supplies to frontline units. The Luftwaffe carried out sorties against Murmansk itself and the Murmansk railway, but the Soviets were always able to repair the damage within a relatively short period of time. It did not take the Germans long to realize that their best chance of disrupting the Murmansk rail line was through commando actions.

The 15th Company, *Brandenburg* Regiment, was selected to undertake this mission (two-thirds of the rank-and-file of the company were Ukrainians, Byelorussians, Volga Germans and Germans from the Balkans and from Tyrol in Austria). Ski troops would be needed, so only the best skiers of the German Army were recruited; including one gold medalist from the 1936 Olympic Games. In addition, the Heereshundeschule (Army Dog School) provided 40 dogs who were suitable for operations in Polar regions. A special training session for the selected dogs focused on training them not to bark and to become motionless on command – even under fire (one wonders how effective this was in combat). Additional Finnish and German specialists were also given to the *Brandenburgers*: two senior German Boy Scouts familiar with the forests of Finland, water-purification specialists, weapons specialists and a meteorological technician. All this took place during the month of October 1941. The *Brandenburgers* also assembled a team of German scientists and specialists who were to design and build special backpacking equipment. Two months later, in late December 1941, the unit was ready.

TRIAL AND ERROR

General Dietl decided to send the unit on a "dry run" in April 1942, to disrupt Soviet rail traffic along the Murmansk rail line between the villages of Alakvetti and Liza. Although the *Brandenburgers* departed as planned, they lacked a proper guide to help them work their way through the thick forests towards the Murmansk line. Tired and demoralized, they decided to abort their mission. The unit were next detailed to stop a Soviet advance near Kiestinki. The exhausted *Brandenburgers* not only played a key role in stopping the Soviet advance, but were also were instrumental in strengthening the Finnish and German defensive positions in the region. In June 1942, they were withdrawn from the frontline and returned to Rovaniemi.

The *Brandenburgers* were willing to try again against the Murmansk line, but not before they had rectified a number of problems that had wrecked the first mission. First, they had lacked rubber boats to cross they mass of Karelian lakes and rivers. Second, authoritative guides were needed, which were now provided by the Finnish military. Even Soviet soldiers who had crossed over to Finnish/German lines (and who volunteered themselves for service) were enlisted.

The *Brandenburgers* were ready for a second attempt on 25 July 1942. Accompanied by seasoned Finnish guides, the *Brandenburgers*, 127 strong, departed from Kuusamo along the Paanajärvi River into central Karelia. Intelligence reported that the Soviets did not have too many troops in their rear areas. This gave a the mission a chance of success, though the men would have to live rough as there was a lack of shelter in northern Karelia. Settlements were sparse. As a precautionary measure, the Luftwaffe ceased flying reconnaissance missions over the target region for fear of alerting the Soviets.

The uniforms of the *Brandenburger* commando team were "sanitized" for this mission: all medals, insignia and other readily identifiable features of Finnish and German militaria were removed. Each trooper was equipped with a pair of rubber boots, a Finnish woodsman's knife (the German ones were left behind) and an ammunition sack. An insect net and insect-repellent was also issued to every man. Because of weight considerations, the 75mm infantry gun was not taken along. As a replacement, every squad received a grenade launcher with ammunition. Aside from the submachine guns, each squad was also given three light machine guns with 2500 round of ammunition for each gun.

Food supplies were also a problem for the undertaking. The forests of Karelia near the arctic circle did not offer much in the way of nourishment. While some wildlife did exist, the *Brandenburgers* did not wish to use their guns to shoot animals for fear of giving their positions away. Thus, food supplies had to be taken along, rationed and dropped off at numerous temporary camps. Ultimately, seven supply camps were established by the advancing team as it made its way to the Murmansk rail line. Each supply camp was then guarded by its three assigned supply troops.

SUCCESS AT LAST

The march to the railway was uneventful, and on 8 August the men reached the the Murmansk line. They placed actuated and timed charges along the rail tracks and as far apart as possible (actuated in that every time a train actuated a switch, it would detonate the charge; also a few of charges were set to go off at random). The *Brandenburgers* were surprised to see no Soviet guards or security precautions along the Murmansk rail line. However, closer reconnaissance revealed that the Soviets did indeed have a guard system in place. From pre-established guard camps, a team of Soviet guards departed from one post, walking along the rail line to the next post, and so on. Having discovered the enemy's security arrangements, the *Brandenburgers* worked around them and set their charges on the line.

A fully loaded Soviet train, coming from Murmansk, hit the first explosive charge (which was placed on an iron bridge). The subse-

German ski troops in the Arctic. With lines of communication – such as railways – so few and distances so great, Soviet lines in the Arctic theatre were easy to infiltrate, making hit-and-run raids by *Brandenburg* units a successful tactic.

quent explosion destroyed the engine and derailed all the wagons. The train with its precious lend-lease goods was lost. A short while later an empty train arrived from the south; it passed over a charge, but the charge was not set to operate on contact. A second empty train arrived shortly thereafter, also from the south. What surprised the Germans observing the whole thing was that the Soviets did not appear at all interested in determining the cause of the accident. Their first and only concern was to repair the rail line as quickly as possible and to salvage as many of the Allied military goods as they could. As more Soviet personnel arrived in the area, the more their repair and salvage activities obliterated the traces of the German charges.

A short while later on the same day, about 9.6km (6 miles) farther up the line, another charge derailed another train. The Soviets sent thousands of NKVD and other troops into the area. NKVD troops shot and executed many civilians who had arrived out of idle curiosity to inspect the scene, suspecting they were saboteurs. Even Red Army soldiers returning from patrol duties were shot on suspicions alone. After the third day, charges were still going off all along the rail line, resulting in more random NKVD shootings against the local population.

Another *Brandenburger* team was located a little farther to the south. It had set most of its charges, but a few still had to be placed. A few of the Russian-speaking *Brandenburgers* disguised themselves as Soviet rail-repair crew members and mingled with the crowd. While pretending to repair rail lines, they were actually able to set additional charges undetected. They even managed to escape the NKVD execution squads who were shooting civilians randomly.

Having done their job, the two small teams made their way back to the town of Rovaniemi. General Dietl was now convinced of the value of his "partisan" units and proceeded to issue medals to his returning heroes.

Far to the south of the Arctic Circle, the *Brandenburgers* were also active in North Africa. Rommel, ever a commander who liked to take risks to achieve results, gave the *Brandenburgers* a free hand in their operational activities, though he did forbid them wearing enemy uniforms. During the month of October 1941, two attempts were made by the *Brandenburgers* to infiltrate Cairo to make contact with Arab nationalists and help them to mount an insurrection against the British. The first attempt to reach Cairo was made via a seaborne infiltration operation. This attempt failed and the team returned to its bases in Libya. The second attempt was to land a team via parachute near Cairo. That also ended in failure. Another team of *Brandenburgers* set out by car and truck, crossing Egypt near the town of Asyut to meet with Arab nationalists. These German-Arab talks included the late Anwar Sadat, who later became the president of Egypt. However, nothing came of these meetings.

Shortly before the capitulation of all German and Italian forces in North Africa in May 1943, the surviving members of the *Brandenburgers* in Africa were withdrawn and brought back to Germany. Their next missions would take them to the Balkans.

British prisoners taken during the attack on Leros in November 1943. As well as British prisoners, the Germans captured 5350 Italians.

BALKAN ADVENTURES

On the 12 september 1943 British forces seized several islands in the Dodecanese, including Samos, Kos and Leros. The occupation of these small islands directly threatened the shipping lanes between the German-occupied island of Rhodes and the mainland of Greece. The British Royal Air Force (RAF) immediately began bombing enemy objectives in Rhodes, the seat of Axis power in the Dodecanese. It also carried out attacks against Crete. The German High Command also feared that these islands may well be used as a forward base by the Allies to invade the Balkans.

Plans were immediately made to recapture these islands from the British. The first of a series of assaults was to take place on the island of Kos (Operation Polar Bear), on 5 October 1943. Kos was chosen as the first objective because it was the only island with an

airfield, which could be used as a forward base for the Luftwaffe in future operations in the Dodecanese. It also prevented the RAF from providing air cover to the other islands, especially Leros, which was next on the list of German objectives in the area. The operation on Kos was carried out successfully by the paratroop company of the *Brandenburg* Regiment, which landed on the island in gliders. Additional forces were supplied from the 22nd Air Landing Division.

The assault on Leros would be the biggest operation in the Dodecanese and the most important due to its harbour facilities. The island was being used by the British as a naval base, a squadron of sea planes were also being operated from Leros, and thus it was a serious threat to German shipping. The operation was codenamed Leopard and would consist of a combined air and seaborne assault.

The day for the start of Operation Leopard was 12 November 1943, and the Luftwaffe had softened up the island's defences for several days in preparation for the assault. The amphibious convoy set off from ports on the east coast of Greece. At dawn on the 12th, Ju 52s took off from an airfield outside Athens for their one-hour flight to Leros. The aircraft approached the island and the paratroops jumped onto the planned landing zone, the flat area of land between the bays – the neck of the island. Before the defenders could react to the landing, the paratroopers were on the ground. The companies were split up and given individual objectives: cutting roads, reconnaissance and providing defensive screens.

VICTORY ON LEROS

On 13 November the Germans succeeded in cutting off the British forces in the north and south, and German reinforcements successfully parachuted in. In the next few days the British mounted several unsuccessful counterattacks against the German positions. The battle for the island was over by the evening of 16 November, with the capture of 3200 British and 5350 Italian troops. German losses had been minimal. The *Brandenburgers* had overcome superior numbers who were backed up by heavy artillery and coastal guns in only four days, and once again the Germans had gained control in the Dodecanese.

The operation on Leros was a great success, but by 1943 the *Brandenburgers* had moved away from strictly covert missions, Leros notwithstanding. Expansion from regiment to division size in late 1942 marked the end of covert operations for this special forces unit and its transformation into a conventional formation. This division saw much action on the Eastern Front, where it was largely destroyed in the great German retreat, but it fought a largely conventional war. The campaigns of the *Brandenburg* Division are outside the scope of this book.

A Failed Elite

Ultimately, Nazi elite units failed to save the Third Reich from destruction. Though they often had resources lavished on them, and were led by some of the finest military commanders in Nazi Germany, they were too small to make a difference. In addition, the the supreme commander of the Third Reich was often guilty of misusing elite units and specialist organizations, which detracted from their overall effectiveness. Adolf Hitler himself must take much of the blame for their demise and defeat.

Despite the ideological drive of the elite SS units, the quality and quantity of enemy resources ranged against them meant that they could not save the Third Reich from military defeat.

Hitler took his fascination with forming elite units and equipping them with wonder weapons to an extreme degree, which may even have actually contributed to Germany losing the war. For example, the concentration of the best leaders, men and weapons in a few elite units robbed the rest of the Wehrmacht of the means to keep fighting. This was most acute in the panzer force, where Hitler's insistence on keeping so-called "fire brigade" units, such as the *Leibstandarte* and *Grossdeutschland* Divisions, up to strength meant that the line panzer divisions were often reduced to going into battle with less than a dozen tanks. This, in turn, created a vicious circle of decline, with frontline panzer divisions unable to hold their sectors and requiring help from the "fire brigades". The more the regular units failed to hold the line, the more Hitler wanted to boost the formations of the Waffen-SS and units like the *Grossdeutschland* Division.

Trained to win the "lightning wars" of 1939–40, Kurt Student's Fallschirmjäger gradually lost their airborne role – and elite status – as German campaigns became more defensive after 1942.

Hitler's love of wonder weapons to equip his elite units was equally disastrous. The amount of scarce raw materials and human resources thrown at the V Weapon programme, the building of monster Tiger II tanks, Me 262s and other weapons, deprived the Wehrmacht of less advanced but more practical hardware. The mass production of these wonder weapons was always ordered before the designs were fully mature or properly tested. Hitler's crazy ideas about weapons production almost brought Germany to its knees in the winter of 1942–43, when production of Panzer IVs was to be discontinued in favour of Panther and Tiger production, even though these tanks were neither ready for action nor able to be produced in the quantities needed. Only the intervention of Albert Speer and General Heinz Guderian put the panzer production plan back on an even keel, and ensured the Wehrmacht had enough tanks to fight in Russia in 1943 and attempt to hold the Normandy Front in 1944.

The proliferation of so-called elite units in the Third Reich owed much to infighting and rivalry among the Nazi hierarchy, rather than

military logic or functional necessity. The ballooning of the Waffen-SS into a force of 39 divisions, for example, was a profligate waste of men and materiel. As an experiment in creating a "European army" for the new Third Reich, Himmler's Waffen-SS was a failure. Nazi racial ideology meant that no attempt was made to recruit foreigners to Germany's cause until it was too late. The half-hearted attempts by Himmler to form an anti-Soviet army of Russians was typical of the attitude of the Nazi leaders. After spending three years exploiting, neglecting or systematically murdering east Europeans as "untermenschen", the attempt by Himmler to recruit these people into the Waffen-SS seems slightly bizarre. Those who did join did so out of desperation. It was usually a choice of signing up to the Waffen-SS or languishing in a concentration camp.

The bulk of these foreign units were raised in eastern Europe and the Balkans during the last two years of the war, and proved to be of very mixed quality. They were excellent counter-insurgency units when fighting on their home territory, but lacked the equipment, training and motivation to take on the best Soviet or Allied troops.

Many German forces fought on to the death – among them the members of the U-boat service, only 10,000 of whom survived the end of the war.

In the closing months of the war, as it became clear that Germany was doomed, the foreigners in the Waffen-SS started to look to the future. While many were looking to save their own skins by escaping from their vengeful fellow countrymen, thousands threw themselves into the fight with renewed vigour. Knowing their fate if Germany lost the war, foreign units such as the *Wiking* Division fought fanatically to hold back the Soviets on the Eastern Front.

Duplication of effort was a complete waste of resources. It may have made sense to the Nazi Party hierarchy who wanted to claim glory and power, but rarely added anything to the military capability of the Third Reich. Skorzeny's commando organization, for example, simply replicated what the Abwehr's *Brandenburg* Division did. Rather than make use of the years of expertise accumulated by the *Brandenburgers*, Skorzeny recruited his own "politically reliable" men and, in the end, the Army's behind-the-lines specialists were converted into a panzergrenadier division, before being sent into the line on the Russian Front.

RIVALRIES AND POLITICS

Rivalry at the top of the Third Reich meant Germany's elite units were never fully employed to the best of their capabilities. Dönitz's U-boats fought the Battle of the Atlantic virtually on their own, for example, because the German submarine chief was not on speaking terms with Luftwaffe chief Hermann Goering.

Nazi elite units and their commanders were showered with medals, publicity and glory to boost the morale of a war-weary German public. While many of these were well earned, the rate at which medals were awarded in the final years of the war tended to devalue them. With the prospect of victory remote and the material resources of the Third Reich obviously exhausted, the continuing lavish distribution of medals seemed gratuitous to hard-bitten combat veterans.

The need for continuing good publicity as defeat followed defeat was one of the main reasons Hitler kept forming new elite units. They filled his need for dramatic action and star personalities. Skorzeny's exploits, for example, were massively hyped at the expense of the real commanders and units that had participated in his missions.

In the end Germany lost the war. Its Führer and his soldiers were defeated in battle by enemies who were prepared to fight with greater determination, bravery and skill. The Soviets and Western Allies eventually learned how to defeat Hitler's war machine, and then mustered the massive economic resources to crush the Third Reich. Hitler got the war of survival he wanted, and he lost. No matter how many elite units he formed, they could not turn the tide of war in Germany's favour. They were just too few in number and often too late on the field of battle to have any lasting impact on the course of the war.

Bibliography

Baker, David, *Messerschmitt Me 262*, Marlborough: Crowood Aviaton Series, 1997.

Bates, H.E., *Flying Bombs over England*, Kent: Froglet Publications, 1994.

Brett-Smith, Richard, *Hitler's Generals*, London: Osprey, 1976.

Carell, Paul, *Scorched Earth*, New York: Ballantine, 1971.

Cooper, Matthew, and Lucas, James, *Panzer*, London: Macdonald, 1976.

Cooper, Matthew, and Lucas, James, *Panzergrenadier*, London: Macdonald and Jane's, 1977.

Cooper, Matthew, and Lucas, James, *Hitler's Elite*, London: Grafton, 1990.

Clark, Alan, *Barbarossa*, New York: William Morrow, 1965.

Cross, Robin, *Citadel: The Battle of Kursk*, London: Michael O'Mara, 1993.

Donald, David, *Warplanes of the Luftwaffe*, London: Aerospace Publishing, 1994.

Downing, David, *The Devil's Virtuosos*, London: New English Library, 1976.

Dunnigan, James, *The Russian Front*, London: Arms and Armour, 1978.

Edwards, Roger, *Panzer: A Revolution in Warfare, 1939–45*, London: Arms and Armour, 1989.

Ellis, Chris, and Chamberlian, Peter, *The 88mm*, London: Parkgate Books, 1998.

Erickson, John, *The Road to Berlin*, London: Weidenfeld & Nicolson, 1983.

Forsyth, Robert, *JV44: The Galland Circus*, Burgess Hill: Classic Publications, 1996.

Glantz, David, *From the Don to the Dnieper*, London: Frank Cass, 1991.

Glantz, David, and House, Jonathan, *When Titans Clashed*, Edinburgh: Birlinn, 2000.

Glantz, David, and House, Jonathan, *The Battle of Kursk*, London: Ian Allan, 1999.

Glantz, David and Orenstein, Harold, *Soviet General Staff: The Battle for Kursk 1943*, London: Frank Cass, 1999.

Guderian, Heinz, *Panzer Leader*, London: Futura, 1979.

Forty, George, *German Tanks of World War Two*, London: Blandford Press, 1987.

Hastings, Max, *Overlord*, London: Michael Joseph, 1984.

History of the Second World War, Paulton: Purnell & Sons Limited, 1966-1974.

Hitler, Adolf, *Hitler's Table Talk*, London: Weidenfeld & Nicolson, 1953.

Irving, David, *The Trail of the Fox*, London: Weidenfeld & Nicolson, 1977.

Jentz, Thomas, Doyle, Hilary and Sarson, Peter, *Tiger I*, London: Osprey, 1993.

Jentz, Thomas, *Panzer Truppen*, Atglen: Schiffer Military History, 1996.

Just, Gunther, and Ulrich, Hans, *Rudel: Stuka Pilot*, Atglen: Schiffer Military History, 1990.

Kaplan, Philip, and Currie, Jack, *Wolfpack*, London: Aurum Press, 1997.

Keegan, John, *Waffen SS: The Asphalt Soldiers*, London: McDonald & Co, 1970.

Kleine, Egon, and Kuhn, Volkmar, *Tiger*, Stuttgart: Motorbuch Verlag, 1990.

Lehman, Rudolf, *The Leibstandarte*, Manitoba: J.J. Fedorowicz, 1990.

Lucas, James, *Kommando: German Special Forces of World War Two*, London: Arms and Armour, 1985.

MacDonald, Charles B, *The Battle of the Bulge*, London: Weidenfeld & Nicolson, 1984.

MacDonald, Charles B, *By Air to Battle*, London: McDonald & Co, 1970.

Manstein, Erich von, *Lost Victories*, London: Methuen, 1958.

Mellenthin, F.W., *Panzer Battles*, London: Futura, 1977.

Mitchell, Samuel, *Hitler's Legions*, London: Leo Cooper, 1985.

Mosley, Leonard, *The Reich Marshal*, London: Weidenfeld & Nicolson, 1974.

Murray, Williamsom, *The Luftwaffe, 1933-1945*, Royston: Eagle Editions, 2000.

Nipe, George, *Decision in the Ukraine*, Manitoba: J.J. Fedorowicz, 1996.

Pallud, Jean Paul, *Battle of the Bulge: Then and Now*, London: After the Battle, 1984.

Price, Alfred, *Luftwaffe*, London: McDonald & Co, 1969.

Ryan, Cornelius, *A Bridge Too Far*, London: Hamish Hamiliton, 1974.

Reynolds, Michael, *Steel Inferno*, Staplehurst: Spellmount, 1997.

Reynolds, Michael, *Men of Steel*, Staplehurst: Spellmount, 1999.

Sadarananda, Dana, *Beyond Stalingrad*, New York: Praeger, 1990.

Seaton, Albert, *The Russo-German War, 1941-45*, New York: Praeger, 1970.

Senger und Etterlin, General Fridio von, *Neither Fear nor Hope*, London: Greenhill, 1989.

Snydor, Charles, *Soldiers of Destruction: The SS Totenkopf Division 1933-45*, Princeton: Princeton University Press, 1977.

Snyder, Louis L., *Encyclopedia of the Third Reich*, Ware: Wordworth Editions, 1976.

Stadler, Silvester, *Die Offensive gegen Kursk 1943*, Osnabruck: Munin Verlag, 1980.

Stroop, Juergen, *The Stroop Report*, London: Secker & Warbourg, 1979.

War Diary of XXXXVIII Panzer Corps, December 1943.

Whiting, Charles, *Hunters from the Sky*, London: Purnell, 1975.

Wilmot, Chester, *Struggle for Europe*, London: Collins, 1952.

Ziemke, Earle F., *Stalingrad to Berlin*, Washington, D.C.: US Government Printing Office, 1968

Ziemke, Earle F. and Bauer, Magna E., *Moscow to Stalingrad*, New York: Military Heritage Press, 1988

Index